AWARENESS
To ACTION

AWARENESS
To ACTION

*The Enneagram,
Emotional Intelligence,
and Change*

ROBERT TALLON and MARIO SIKORA

Scranton: University of Scranton Press

Library of Congress Cataloging-in-Publication Data

Tallon, Robert, 1947 –
    Awareness to action : the enneagram, emotional intelligence, and change : a guide to improving performance / by Robert Tallon and Mario Sikora.
        p. cm.
Includes bibliographical references and index.
ISBN 1-58966-125-7(pbk.)
    1.   Enneagram.   2.   Emotional intelligence.   I. Sikora, Mario, 1963 - .
    II. Title.

BF698.35.E54T35 2003
155.2'6—dc22   2003064533

Distribution:

University of Scranton Press
Chicago Distribution Center
11030 South Langley Avenue
Chicago   IL   60628

In memory of Andrew J. Tallon
and
Paul W. Moore

ACKNOWLEDGMENTS

For Robert

Thanks to Dennis Tallon, Andy Tallon, Dave Walling, Tom Forst, Steve Metzman, Lee Metzman, Patricia Wintyr, Suzanne Baldino Jones, Mark Heisler, Dave Beswick, Rico Provasoli, Bob Zuercher, and Don Johnson, for their friendship, support, and encouragement.

Thanks to my children, Aaron and Lauren, for their love and patience, especially when I said, "Soon," in response to their weekly question, "How's the book coming?"

Special thanks to Lois Miller-Tallon, who lived through the eight years of starts, stops, and ongoing challenges that characterized this book. Her encouragement, counsel, and personal support were invaluable.

Thanks to my co-author, Mario Sikora, whose insight, precision, dedication to scholarship, and relentless energy were essential in creating this book.

Lastly, thanks to my wife, Robyn, whose mantra, "If you could only see yourself the way I see you," reminded me to believe in myself. She caught me when I fell; fed me when I forgot to eat; gave me air when I could not catch my breath; and loved me no matter what.

For Mario

First, thanks are due to all of my clients, from whom I have learned just about everything I know about the Enneagram; especially Ed Zakrzewski, who provided a forum and who saw the value of this work before anyone else did.

Thanks to my co-author, Bob Tallon, who introduced me to the Enneagram and was a great partner for this project. Bob was thoughtful, meticulous, and passionate about this book.

Thanks are due to Lois Miller-Tallon, who was unwavering in her support and could always be counted on to provide perspective.

Thanks to Dennis and Donna Tallon, thoughtful and supportive voices both.

Thanks to my sons, Adrian, Alec, and Alexie, who fill me with awe and are my unbridled joy.

Most importantly, thanks to my wife, Tanya, who takes my breath away. She is my most trusted advisor, my most reliable sounding board, and she always knows exactly what to say.

CONTENTS

Take *Awareness to Action* to the next level...

Download the
FREE expanded version of
The Awareness to Action
Emotional Competency Assessment (ECA)
A 360-degree assessment tool
with developmental guide
at
www.awarenesstoaction.com.

Download the
FREE
Leadership Competency
360-Degree Assessment
at
www.awarenesstoaction.com.

Check out additional
Performance Improvement
resources at
www.awarenesstoaction.com

HOW TO USE THIS BOOK

Awareness to Action presents a powerful model for understanding personality types, their relationship to emotional intelligence, and a precise method for improving performance. There is always a temptation when reading a book such as this to skip over the beginning chapters and go right to the section on your personality type, especially if you are already familiar with the Enneagram. We encourage you to read Chapters One and Two before reading any of the subsequent chapters. Our goal was to structure this book as a resource that could be returned to again and again. Thus, we have written the chapters that cover the individual personality types as a guidebook rather than a narrative. Chapter One explains the format and the basic concepts behind the Enneagram and by reading it first you will gain more from the chapter on your type. Chapter Two, on The Awareness to Action Process, explains the method for improving performance that is demonstrated in each type chapter. The corresponding section in each type chapter may not be clear to those who skip Chapter Two.

If you are not familiar with your personality type, we encourage you to complete the assessment found in Chapter Three. The assessment will help you identify your personality type and point you to the chapter that will be most useful to you.

We felt that some material that would be helpful did not quite fit into the main body of the book, so we created five appendices.

Appendix A provides a 360-degree assessment of the emotional competencies found in this book along with a developmental guide for improving in each of the 16 competencies.

Appendix B gives general recommendations for growth for the nine types. These tips cover a broader area than the competencies found in the book, and address common weaknesses of each type.

Appendix C provides a sample action plan, and the text walks you through the process of creating an effective action plan.

Appendix D provides some additional insight into identifying your personality type by comparing your behavior to a set of performance derailers that tend to bedevil each of the types.

Appendix E describes how we applied the concept of the strategies to Jack Welch's "4E plus P" leadership competency model and to a basic sales competency model.

PROLOGUE: THE BIRTH OF A BOOK

We don't receive wisdom; we must discover it for ourselves after a
journey that no one can spare us.
MARCEL PROUST

The concepts presented in *Awareness to Action* were developed and refined in organizations, at public workshops, and during private coaching sessions by the authors over the past 15 years. Some of the concepts were published in a variety of periodicals. We received feedback from a surprisingly wide variety of clients, workshop participants, and readers—business executives, consultants, healthcare workers, psychologists, and general readers from across the US and around the world. People from countries including South Africa, Australia, Thailand, Brazil, and the United Kingdom wrote to share their enthusiasm for our approach to the Enneagram and to encourage us to write a book about it.

The feedback we received centered on these themes:

- People found our approach to be positive in its depiction of the personality types, focusing on the positive as well as the negative and pointing to improvement rather than dwelling on dysfunction.

- They found the way we formatted and taught the material useful for easy reference; they could return to it again and again to gain new insights into their behavior and that of their co-workers.

- The Awareness to Action Process is a simple but extremely effective model for growth.

- Finally, people found that the concept of the "strategies," the central theme at the heart of each personality type, was a clear and precise way to understand the differences they saw in the people around them.

It is this concept that we have found most rewarding and useful in our work as well, and served as the impetus to write this book.

When we began what was to become *Awareness to Action* in 2000, our idea was to simply tie the idea of emotional intelligence with what we then knew of the Enneagram. As work progressed, we kept being confronted by both variation and consistency within the types. That is, people of a given type both shared common traits and showed marked differences. As we closely examined what was at the heart of the commonalities we began to home in on what was at the core of "type": a central theme or patterned "way of being in the world" that influenced a person's thoughts, feelings, and behaviors. After much debate, we settled on the word "strategy" to describe this theme or pattern since it is a person's way of navigating their world.

Working with the Enneagram in terms of strategies rather than traits has transformed our work. Seeing the nine types of the Enneagram in terms of "shared traits" (as most authors do) often leads to confusion and mistyping. Much of the Enneagram literature describes the types in terms of *what they are like* ("Nines are peaceful, easygoing, calm," etc.) instead of *why they do what they do* ("Nines may avoid conflict or self-deprecate because they strive to be peaceful").

Descriptions of traits can be valuable (and we provide such descriptions in this volume), but they do not account for why, for example, Nines can sometimes be combative and argumentative or why other people of other types can sometimes appear to avoid conflict or exhibit other "Nine-ish" behaviors.

Focusing on the strategies explains these discrepancies. Above all, Nines are striving to be peaceful. This generally leads them to be easygoing and calm, but sometimes they are combative when their inner peace is disrupted. To us, the strategy is at the heart of "type." The traits exhibited by people of a given type are merely logical manifestations of the strategy. They are generally consistent, but by no means fixed.

Not only is this approach more accurate—it is more optimistic and liberating: You are not your *type*; you simply have a habitual strategy for being in the world and you can change your behaviors if you follow the three steps of the Awareness to Action Process.

Focusing on the strategies has also allowed us to apply the Enneagram to a variety of competency models for leadership, sales, executive coaching, and team building. It becomes relatively easy to clearly observe, classify, and predict tendencies in any set of competencies when you have studied the strategies and how they influence peoples' behavior.

Clients have asked us to use this insight to help their employees improve in a wide variety of competency models. A brief description of how we did this for a leadership model and a sales model is provided in Appendix E.

Hearing feedback from our clients and readers has been a great opportunity for us to refine our work. Learning how readers have used our approach to improve their professional and personal lives has been profoundly rewarding and has also allowed us to develop friendships with people from across the globe. We would love to hear your stories and any feedback you might have on this book's content. Feel free to contact us through our website: www.awarenesstoaction.com.

INTRODUCTION

It is not the strongest of the species that survives, nor the most intelligent, but the one most responsive to change.
CHARLES DARWIN

This book is about emotional intelligence and personality type; more specifically, it is about improving performance in 16 emotional competencies that have been linked to excellence at work, in relationships, and other aspects of life. It examines:

- What these competencies are,
- How your particular personality type relates to your tendencies to be strong or weak in each of them, and
- How you can make positive changes to strengthen your performance in these competencies and in emotional intelligence in general.

What is Emotional Intelligence?

The term "emotional intelligence" has become very popular lately, due in large part to the work of Daniel Goleman, David McClelland, and others. *Emotional intelligence* is generally understood to be the ability to:

- Identify your emotions and manage your responses to them. (For example, recognizing that you are angry with a coworker but not giving in to the temptation to yell at him.)
- Identify the emotions of others and manage your responses to them. (For example, recognizing that a coworker is angry with you but not giving in to the temptation to escalate the conflict.)

Why Improve Emotional Intelligence?

How important is emotional intelligence compared to technical skills and intellect for excellence at work? Why do smart people fail? What are the most sought after skills in new employees? Studies conducted from 1982 to the present indicate the overwhelming importance of emotional intelligence.

- More than 2,000 managers from 12 large organizations were analyzed to determine the most important competencies for success. Eighty-one percent of the competencies that distinguished outstanding managers were related to emotional intelligence. (Boyatzis, 1982)
- In a study of 181 different positions from 121 organizations worldwide 67% of the abilities deemed essential for effective performance were emotional competencies. (Rosier, 1994)
- In analyzing data from 40 different corporations to differentiate star performers from average performers, emotional competencies were found to be twice as important in contributing to excellence as pure intellect and expertise. (Jacobs and Chen, 1997)

Repeatedly, in all categories of jobs and in all kinds of organizations, studies show that once a baseline of intelligence and expertise are met, *emotional competence* mattered *at least twice as much* as additional IQ and technical expertise. Improvement in emotional intelligence means improvement in effectiveness at work and in other spheres of life.

The Key to Improved Performance

There is an essential factor that is often overlooked when you try to improve your performance in any area—*your habitual thoughts and behaviors*. This book explores nine specific strategies for dealing with life and the impact that these strategies have on your thoughts and behaviors. These strategies form the foundation for the nine distinct and identifiable personality types. In the pages that follow, we will discuss how each of these strategies helps and hinders you, and how you can better capitalize on your particular strategy's strengths and overcome its weaknesses. We will explore how each strategy is valuable when used in the right context but can limit your ability to perform well when used in the wrong situation, habitually, or without awareness.

The Enneagram Theory of Personality

The model we use for identifying the personality types and their related strategies is called the *Enneagram* (pronounced "ANY-a-gram"). The Enneagram diagram consists of a triangle and a six-sided figure enclosed within a circle. These elements combine to create nine points along the circle (see Figure 1). Though no one is sure when the first enneagram was drawn, it is thought to have its roots in ancient Greece—thus its name (*ennea* is Greek for *nine*; *gram* means *drawing*). In the early 1970s, the application of this diagram to understanding personality began to grow in popularity, namely through the work of Claudio Naranjo, M.D., a noted Gestalt psychologist. Over time, numerous schools of thought sprang from Naranjo's work, and there are currently many books available on the *Enneagram of personality* (as it came to be known).

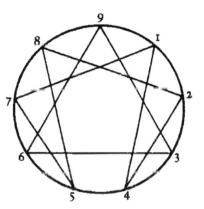

Figure 1. The Enneagram

This book describes our understanding of the Enneagram of personality. It is based on observations gleaned from working with hundreds of business clients and workshop attendees over the past decade. The book explores the root motivations behind personality type, identifies how each type behaves in the Enneagram Emotional Competencies, and charts a path for personal growth and performance improvement for each of the nine types. It addresses the practical concerns of people interested in performance in the workplace. We have used the Enneagram as a tool to help individuals and teams improve performance in organizations as diverse as family-owned businesses, government agencies, and Fortune 500 companies. It is the most accurate and useful tool available for understanding personality type, developing self-awareness, and increasing effectiveness.

It is important to distinguish three terms that will be used through out this book: *enneagram point*, *strategy*, and *personality type*. By *enneagram point* we mean the actual position of a given point or number on the enneagram diagram. By *strategy*, we are referring to the nine ways of interacting with the world that correspond to the nine points. For example, the *strategy* of Striving to be Outstanding is found at *Point* Three of the enneagram. *Personality type* refers to the collection of attitudes and behaviors that result from reliance on the *strategy*. Thus, a *Type* Three is one who exhibits the traits (such as self-assurance and goal-orientation) of a person whose Preferred Strategy is Striving to be Outstanding. For the sake of simplicity, throughout this book we will refer to examples of the personality types by their numbers, i.e., "Nines," "Ones," "Sevens," etc.

The word "striving" is also significant. When we say that a person or a particular personality type is "striving to be" something, we are referring to a feeling that they are trying to recapture, a sense of self that drives them, and an identity that they are trying to project to others. It does not mean that they have necessarily accomplished this, however. The Three in our example above strives to be outstanding, but has flaws and shortcomings just like the rest of us.

Following are brief descriptions of the nine personality types of the Enneagram that identify the chief drive of each type—i.e., what they strive to be—and the quality the type resists most strongly—i.e., what they strive *not* to be.

Type One: Ones strive to be perfect and work hard not to be irresponsible or careless.

Type Two: Twos strive to be connected to others and work hard not to be physically or emotionally isolated.

Type Three: Threes strive to be outstanding and work hard not to be mediocre or average.

Type Four: Fours strive to be unique and work hard not to be plain, typical, or mundane.

Type Five: Fives strive to be detached and work hard not to be reckless, emotional, and uncontrolled.

Type Six: Sixes strive to be secure and work hard not to let their guard down and be passive.

Type Seven: Sevens strive to be excited and work hard not to be bored or boring.

Type Eight: Eights strive to be powerful and work hard not to be vulnerable or dependent on others.

Type Nine: Nines strive to be peaceful and work hard not to bring attention to themselves or their needs.

The Habitual Patterns of Personality

The word "personality" comes from the Latin word "persona," which means "mask." Your personality is the face you wear in public and the image you prefer to have of yourself in private. It is a specific set of habitual attitudes and their resultant behaviors that influences your beliefs, opinions, and interactions with others.

The way you develop your personality is a complicated topic worthy of a separate book of its own. For the sake of *this* book, suffice it to say that humans are a remarkably efficient species and the personality is a way of simplifying and organizing life. You focus on a *strategy* early in life—a system of behaviors and attitudes that serve you well—and you stick to it. This strategy allows you to create generalizations about life and these generalizations make life easier. Situations you encounter can quickly be compared to other situations you have encountered and you can comfortably fall back on the solutions that have worked for you in the past. This approach works fine until the generalization is inaccurate and your "tried-and-true" solution no longer works. When you are able to adapt your behaviors in such an instance (that is, try a new solution), you are acting effectively. However, you are often unable to adapt and tend to cling to your strategy and force it to fit your circumstances. You *overdo* your strategy and it becomes restricting and limiting—the peace-seeking Nine becomes passive and avoids necessary confrontation; the security-seeking Six refuses to take chances and settles for mediocre performance; the excitement-seeking Seven becomes distracted and unfocused, etc.

This book explores the relationship between these nine distinct personality types and emotional intelligence. It shows how you can use the awareness of your own personality type to become more effective and successful in your work, your relationships, and your life.

CHAPTER 1

THE ENNEAGRAM: AN OVERVIEW

Everyone is necessarily the hero of his own life story.
JOHN BARTH

The Enneagram presented in this book is the authors' interpretation of the more traditional Enneagram of personality. It is a robust and sophisticated model of personality; it is also fairly simple, primarily consisting of a few basic components. These components are explained in this chapter, except for The Awareness to Action Process, which is explained in Chapter Two. These components are:

- *The Type at a Glance;*
- *Each Type's Preferred, Neglected, and Support Strategies;*
- *The Enneagram Emotional Competencies; and*
- *The Awareness to Action Process*

The Type at a Glance

Each chapter that describes a personality type (Chapters 4 through 12) includes a section called "At a Glance," that includes 13 categories. Some of these categories cover typical issues that impact performance, such as "Belief About Work," "How They Frustrate Others," and "Approach to Problem Solving." Other categories, such as "Defensive Routine" and "Where They Shine," will help you identify people of that personality type.

The Nine Strategies

Each of the nine points on the Enneagram represents a strategy for interacting with the environment that has an influence on personality. (See Table 1 for definitions of the nine strategies.) You have access to each of these strategies and, ideally, would draw upon and apply them when the situation warrants it. However, when you are stuck in your habitual personality patterns you tend to rely on a favored strategy (what we call the *Preferred Strategy*) regardless of the situation, believing that this strategy is the solution to all of your challenges and problems. The objective of using the Enneagram is to help you see the limitations of over-relying on these habitual patterns and to help you expand your behavioral choices to include more flexible—and effective—actions.

While you would do best to apply the strategies without preference in response to the specific situation you are facing, doing so is very difficult. A more realistic goal is to gradually broaden your internal definition of your Preferred Strategy to accommodate behaviors that do not yet come naturally for you. For example, Eights, whose Preferred Strategy is *Striving to be Powerful*, tend to be forceful and aggressive when they are trying to influence others. They may be easily frustrated, and their frustration may cause them to be loud and intimidating. When they receive feedback that they need to be less aggressive, Eights often struggle to implement the change because their current understanding of what it means to be "powerful" tells them that being aggressive is good. Eights will begin to improve in this area when they are able to broaden their definition of what it means to be powerful so that it includes less-aggressive behaviors.

As your definitions of your Preferred Strategy expands to include a wider range of behaviors and attitudes, you move from being *efficient* (doing things economically and quickly) to being *effective* (doing the *right* things economically and quickly). This broader understanding of the strategy begins to loosen the strategy's hold on you and, eventually, the other strategies begin to feel more comfortable and you find yourself using them more. The peaceful Nine begins to feel more confident and strives to be outstanding; the detached Five begins to strive to be powerful; and so on.

TABLE 1: The Nine Strategies

Strategy at Point One	**Striving to be Perfect**—The desire to be flawless, good, and to feel that everything is right with you and the world.
Strategy at Point Two	**Striving to be Connected**—The desire to be appreciated and to be deeply united with others and with your own feelings.
Strategy at Point Three	**Striving to be Outstanding**—The desire to stand out as an exemplary member of the group and to be seen as valuable, successful, and accomplished.
Strategy at Point Four	**Striving to be Unique**—The desire to be different, autonomous, creative, and to be understood and appreciated for your special qualities.
Strategy at Point Five	**Striving to be Detached**—The desire to be autonomous, independent, and able to find serenity with your own thoughts.
Strategy at Point Six	**Striving to be Secure**—The desire to be safe and a part of a group, cause, or philosophy; to trust others and your own judgment.
Strategy at Point Seven	**Striving to be Excited**—The desire to be stimulated, happy, enthusiastic, to have fun, and to inspire others.
Strategy at Point Eight	**Striving to be Powerful**—The desire to be strong, to take action, and to be able to express your will, influence, and vitality.
Strategy at Point Nine	**Striving to be Peaceful**—The desire to be in harmony with your world, other people, and your own thoughts; to be calm and relaxed.

Strategies, Influences, and Traits

It is important to understand the difference between *strategies*, *influences*, and *traits* as they are used in this book.

The discussion of the *strategies* and each personality type's unique relationship to them is the only topic in this book that should be considered to be true *in every case*. That is, the *strategies* describe inner motivations and apply to everyone of that personality type. The *strategies* can be seen as what define the personality type—a Four, by definition, strives to be unique; a Six strives to be secure, etc. If Striving to be Unique is not something that is central to your approach to life, you are not a Four, even if you have some "Four-ish" traits.

The other sections, such as the Type at a Glance and The Enneagram Emotional Competencies, describe the general *traits and tendencies* of each type that apply to *most* people of that type, but perhaps not to all people of that type.

Human beings are very complicated creatures and each of us has personality traits that are affected by a number of environmental *influences*. These *influences* include cultural, family, and socio-economic background; psychological health; emotional intelligence; and so on. These *influences* cause us all to act out our strategies in different ways, so people of the same personality type may exhibit different *traits*. Some Sixes are loud and aggressive, while others are quiet and timid; all Sixes, however, are Striving to be Secure. Some Nines are outgoing and assertive, while others are quiet and withdrawn; but all Nines are Striving to be Peaceful.

Therefore, it is important not to make universal statements about the *traits* of each type. For example, many Nines enjoy nature, gardening, and the outdoors; but certainly not all of them do. To understand the types—both your own and others'—focus on the *strategies,* and see the *traits* as common, but not universal, manifestations of the *strategies*.

"At Their Best," "Typically," and "When Stressed"

Throughout this book we refer to how the personality types appear when they are "at their best," "typically," or "when stressed."

"At Their Best"

When you are at your best—that is, when you are relaxed, comfortable, and secure—you are less in the grip of your habitual patterns. You tend to be more flexible, responding naturally and appropriately to what life brings your way. At your best you are exhibiting the most appropriate behavior of your personality type and avoiding the pitfalls of your habitual behaviors.

One of the hallmarks of a person at his or her best is *balance*. For example, the balanced Two is connected with others but not needy or codependent, assertive but not demanding or manipulative, and autonomous without feeling isolated or unappreciated. Likewise, the balanced Four is unique without feeling flawed and misunderstood, he feels content just as he is without feeling the need to be critical of others, and connected to others without feeling that he must find a sense of wholeness through another person.

"Typically"

However, if you are like most people you don't always perform or behave at your best; most of the time you are in some way affected by your habitual patterns, though not necessarily in negative ways. In fact, the strategies, even when habitual, often serve you well. The Three who habitually strives to be outstanding often thrives in the workplace and motivates others through her shining example; the Nine who strives to be peaceful is often a comforting and reassuring presence in an organization; and the Eight who strives to be powerful can often push a project through a difficult time. It is this "most of the time" that is described in the paragraphs on "typical" behavior. The word "typically," refers to examples of people who are applying their habitual patterns in ways that are basically useful but not necessarily optimal.

"When Stressed"

When this book refers to behavior that occurs "when stressed," it is describing behavior that is usually counterproductive. Stress causes people to become defensive. When you are defensive you are quicker to go on autopilot to unconsciously rely on behaviors and attitudes that you think have worked for you in the past and that support your sense of who you are. When these strategies don't work, stress builds. Rather than stepping back and trying another way to accomplish what you want, stress causes you to fall further into your old habits and to do them *even more*, whatever they may be—becoming *more* forceful, withdrawing *further,* becoming *more* rigid, etc. Stress causes each personality type to distort the Preferred Strategy and behave in a specific and predictable way. For example, stress causes the outstanding Three to become *attention seeking* and self-centered, the peaceful Nine to be unresponsive and *passive*, and the powerful Eight to be *uncontrolled* and domineering. It is important to understand the distortion of your Preferred Strategy because it causes behavior that, if not held in check, will get you into trouble over and over again.

The stress response—overdoing and distorting your Preferred Strategy—often helps you accomplish your immediate goal, but usually at some price. It may help to draw an analogy using three different kinds of carpenters. Think of the strategies as tools in a carpenter's tool belt, and the three stages of personality ("At Their Best," Typically," and "When Stressed") as three types of carpenters: *an expert carpenter, an average carpenter*, and *an unskilled carpenter. An expert carpenter* knows that each tool has an appropriate function: a hammer for driving nails, a saw for cutting wood, a wrench for tightening nuts, etc., and he uses them accordingly. *An average carpenter* will favor a particular tool and use it for tasks that it was not particularly designed for, but for which the tool makes a convenient substitute, such as using a hammer to wedge a board into place. *An unskilled carpenter,* however, will become enamored of a particular tool—such as a hammer—and reflexively reach for that tool each time he faces a task, whether the task is driving a nail or cutting wood.

A person "at their best" is analogous to the expert carpenter who uses the right tool for the right job, a person behaving "typically" is like the average carpenter, and a person "when stressed" is like the unskilled carpenter—the one trying to cut wood with a hammer.

The Preferred Strategy

The strategy adopted by your personality type is called the *Preferred Strategy* because it is a *preference* rather than an absolute fixture. That is, while it is the strategy that you are most comfortable with, it is not the only one to which you have access. You have access to all of the strategies to a greater or lesser extent, but try to make life simpler by relying primarily on one of them.

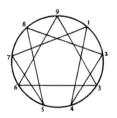

The Neglected Strategy

As seen on the Enneagram, each point is connected to two other points by the internal lines of the diagram. Each personality type is hampered by a distrust of the strategy found at one of the points connected to it, tending to focus on the distorted version of that strategy rather than seeing its value. This distrust causes you to "neglect" the strategy—seeing it as too risky to *comfortably* include in the normal behavioral repertoire.

The distrust occurs because the two strategies are in some way contradictory. For example, Fives prefer the strategy of Striving to be Detached. They see the strategy at Point Eight, Striving to be Powerful (which implies being assertive and actively engaging in life), as contradicting their desire to be detached. Fives will tend to focus on how being powerful can lead to being uncontrolled and neglect that strategy and many of the behaviors associated with it.

This does not mean that you *never* use the Neglected Strategy. However, you tend to under-use it, and your personality type colors your application of it when you do use it. The Five may at times strive to be powerful, but he will do it in a "Five-ish" way. He may prefer to serve as the leader's advisor rather than be the actual leader, or he may wield power through the control of information rather than through force of personality.

Similarly, Ones will focus on the *distortion* of the strategy found at Point Seven—Striving to be Excited. Ones strive to be perfect and resist losing their composure and possibly making mistakes. They therefore see the strategy of Striving to be Excited as a dangerous one and they tend to focus on its distortion: irresponsibility.

Your ability to grow is greatly enhanced by your willingness to confront and correct this misunderstanding and become more comfortable with the Neglected Strategy. For example, an Eight tends to be uncomfortable with the strategy found at Point Two—Striving to be Connected. Rather than fully benefit from the experience of connecting deeply with others, Eights believe that trying to do so will make them dependent on others. Thus they tend to keep people at arm's length, except for those inside their close circle. They hide their own vulnerabilities under a protective armor of strength and assertiveness. Eight's grow when they realize that they can be both powerful and connected, and that being connected doesn't necessarily mean that they will be dependent.

...*Except when the opposite is true: The Contradiction*

To truly understand the interplay between the Preferred Strategy and the Neglected Strategy, it is important to look at a dynamic we call "the Contradiction." It is a basic psychological principle that any quality that is ignored or repressed will be acted out surreptitiously.

For example, the milquetoast office-worker who passively absorbs his boss's scorn all day may fly into a fit of road rage on the drive home. In the same way, each personality type will occasionally exhibit the very traits it is trying to avoid or suppress. The nonconforming Four who strives to be unique will rigidly expect others to follow rules and guidelines the Four thinks are important—behavior often seen in Ones. The humble and self-deprecating Nine will find subtle (and sometimes not-so-subtle) ways to have her demands met.

This contradictory behavior will usually occur in an environment in which the person is comfortable and secure. Many people will deny and/or be unable to see that this contradictory behavior takes place because it is out of character with their self-image; others will be more aware of the behavior. People in this latter group often struggle with identifying with a particular personality type because they see both sides of their contradictory nature.

The Support Strategy

The second connecting point is called the "Support Strategy" because this particular strategy serves to reinforce your Preferred Strategy or serve as an alternative response when the Preferred Strategy is not effective. The Support Strategy can be used to either enhance your effectiveness when you are at your best or keep you struck right where you are when you are under stress. For example, Twos use Striving to be Powerful (found at Point Eight) to reinforce being connected. Twos can do so positively by using their relationships and energy to help others accomplish their goals, but they can also do it in a negative way by angrily manipulating others to make the changes they feel the other person should make. Type Three uses peacefulness to reinforce being outstanding by cultivating an air of effortless grace that bespeaks their ability to be successful, but they may also hide behind a façade of composure while feeling insecure and seeking cues from others on how to think, feel, or act.

The Enneagram Emotional Competencies

An *emotional competency* is a specific capability based on emotional intelligence that makes you more successful in interacting with your world. The Enneagram Emotional Competencies are a set of 16 emotional competencies that measure emotional intelligence. They are separated into two broad categories: personal competencies and social competencies, which are further separated into four narrower categories: Self-Awareness, Self-Management, Attunement to Others, and Relationship Building. The *personal competencies,* such as self-awareness and self-control, relate to our ability to manage and constructively use our emotions; the *social competencies*, such as empathy and communication, relate to our ability to recognize emotional states in others and use the information to work toward common benefit.

This book explores in depth the strengths and weaknesses of each personality type in relationship to each of these 16 emotional competencies—with the goal of improving performance in weaker competencies.

The 16 Enneagram Emotional Competencies are:

PERSONAL COMPETENCIES

Self-Awareness

Self-Awareness: ability to identify one's thought processes, emotions, and skills
Self-Confidence: confidence in one's powers and abilities

Self-Management

Self-Control: restraint exercised over one's impulses, emotions, or desires
Adaptability: flexibility in handling change
Trustworthiness: maintaining standards of honesty and integrity
Optimism: ability to anticipate and expect the best possible outcome
Initiative: readiness to act on opportunities
Achievement Drive: striving to meet or improve a standard of excellence
Resiliency: capacity to endure in the face of obstacles

SOCIAL COMPETENCIES

Attunement to Others

Empathy: awareness of and participation in others' feelings, ideas, and needs

Political Awareness: reading a group's emotional currents and power relationships
Communication: listening openly and sending convincing messages

Relationship Building

Cooperation: working with others toward shared goals
Leadership: inspiring and leading individuals and groups
Influence: wielding effective tactics for persuasion
Conflict Management: negotiating and resolving disputes

Emotions are an uncomfortable topic in many workplaces and they are often only addressed when they are displayed in inappropriate ways. It is important to understand that emotional intelligence in general, and in this book in particular, is not about becoming *more* emotional or eliminating or controlling your emotions. It is about managing the behaviors that result from emotions. You cannot control or eliminate your emotions, nor should you want to. Emotions are a critical part of your ability to function in the world; they serve as an early warning system that prepares responses to circumstances that your conscious awareness may not have fully processed. For example, the emotion of fear keeps you from walking into dark alleys, and the emotion of excitement readies you for action. Emotions can also be enjoyable, and life without them would feel dry and unsatisfying. The goal of working with the Enneagram Emotional Competencies is to understand the way emotions affect performance and to learn to use these competencies to your advantage.

This becomes easier when you understand the connection between personality type and emotional intelligence. The traits, preferences, and limitations of your personality type combine to affect your ability in the competencies in predictable ways. For instance, Twos, who strive to be connected, and Sixes, who strive to be secure, generally thrive in the competency of cooperation, but Fives, who strive to be detached, and Fours, who strive to be unique, may struggle in that competency. You must first understand your attitudes and patterns of behavior before you can successfully improve your performance in these areas.

CHAPTER 2

THE AWARENESS TO ACTION PROCESS—THE PATH TO PERFORMANCE IMPROVEMENT

Intentions count as nothing if we do not translate them into action.
MARSHA SINETAR

Understanding your personality type—your Preferred Strategy and the attitudes and behaviors that stem from it—leads to improved performance in the 16 emotional competencies. This understanding is

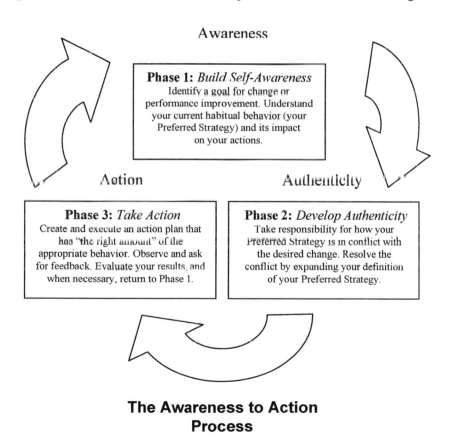

Awareness

Phase 1: *Build Self-Awareness*
Identify a goal for change or performance improvement. Understand your current habitual behavior (your Preferred Strategy) and its impact on your actions.

Action

Authenticity

Phase 3: *Take Action*
Create and execute an action plan that has "the right amount" of the appropriate behavior. Observe and ask for feedback. Evaluate your results, and when necessary, return to Phase 1.

Phase 2: *Develop Authenticity*
Take responsibility for how your Preferred Strategy is in conflict with the desired change. Resolve the conflict by expanding your definition of your Preferred Strategy.

The Awareness to Action Process

converted to performance by applying the three steps of The Awareness to Action Process: Build Self-Awareness, Develop Authenticity, and Take Action.

The Awareness to Action Process starts with establishing a general goal for change in one or more of the competencies, and works toward identifying and completing specific action steps for building more-effective behaviors that fall within that competency.

Phase One: Build Self-Awareness

Phase One of the process is Build Self-Awareness—seeing your current behaviors and attitudes and understanding their roots and the affect they have on your performance, relationships, and personal satisfaction—is the bedrock of growth or improvement in any endeavor. Once you identify a goal in any area (such as improving your serve in tennis), you must take stock of where you currently stand in relation to that goal and why. ("My serve usually goes into the net when my ball toss is too low.") The same applies to improvement in the emotional competencies. If you want to improve in the competency of communication, you must first take stock of the gap between your current communication habits and attitudes about communication and identify the communication skills you wish to have.

The Awareness to Action Process shows you how to build self-awareness by exploring your Preferred Strategy and understanding its impact on your performance.

Your Preferred Strategy colors everything about you. It influences your beliefs and the content of your thoughts: Sixes, who strive to be secure, tend to see the world as a threatening place and devote a great deal of mental energy to ferreting out potential dangers and hidden motives; Nines, who strive to be peaceful, generally do not.

Your Preferred Strategy influences your behavior: Sevens, who strive to be excited, tend to be outgoing, spontaneous, and, at times, hyperactive; Ones, who strive to be perfect, tend to be controlled and deliberate.

Finally, your Preferred Strategy influences the expression of your emotions: Twos, who strive to be connected, are usually comfortable demonstrating both joy and sadness; Eights, who strive to be powerful, are often guarded with their emotions.

The other components of the Enneagram described in Chapter One—the Neglected Strategy, the Contradiction, and the Support

Strategy—are essentially dictated by the Preferred Strategy. (For example, Ones *neglect* "excitement" because it is in conflict with their true desire, Striving to be Perfect.) While it is useful to explore the impact of these components on your performance, it is best to view this work as a refinement of the work you do around your Preferred Strategy. Focusing on the Preferred Strategy first and understanding the hold it has on you will be most beneficial.

Each chapter addresses three emotional competencies that the personality type covered in that chapter would do well to improve in. Further, the chapter demonstrates how The Awareness to Action Process can be used to improve performance in one specific competency. It is important to view the suggestions made in the chapters as recommendations rather than rules. True effectiveness involves identifying and improving in the competencies that are most important for you right now. If you have recently been promoted to a management position, for example, it may be best for you to focus on improving in the competency of leadership, even if that competency is not highlighted in the chapter on your personality type. The process demonstrated in the chapter can serve as a guide to working with the other competencies.

Building self-awareness, while a critical step in any performance improvement effort, is not enough—it is simply too easy to continue to fall back into the grip of your habitual patterns. Therefore, it is necessary to move to Phase Two of The Awareness to Action Process—*Develop Authenticity*.

Phase Two: Develop Authenticity

Develop Authenticity means being honest about and consistent in your motivations, beliefs, and values. It involves recognizing and taking responsibility for your behavior rather than ignoring or denying it, rationalizing it, or blaming others for it. This phase has two parts: 1) identifying the conflict between your Preferred Strategy and the change you are trying to make and 2) reframing your definition of the strategy so it can include new behaviors.

There is an important caveat that must be made here: You cannot and will not change until you realize that you—and only you—are responsible for your actions; not your mother, not society, not the school system, not your spouse and co-workers. In addition, only you can make the changes you wish to see. You will not change when your co-workers change, or when your spouse and friends and boss start treating you better; you will change when you decide to do the hard work involved in changing a behavior.

A critical part of taking responsibility is honesty. You cannot change or improve performance until you are honest with yourself (and others) and admit that there is room for growth. You must be willing to objectively look at yourself and be honest about your current strengths and weaknesses, and be willing to do something about them.

Identifying and reconciling the conflict between your Preferred Strategy and the change you are trying to make is critical because: 1) you probably do not realize that there *is* a conflict, and 2) you may not see how the conflict undermines attempts to change.

Most people, when confronted about a problem behavior and pressed for an explanation, will respond with something along the lines of "that's just how I am." The truth, however, is that you do everything for a reason. You do the things you claim you would like to stop doing because you get rewarded for them. This reward is generally that the current behavior helps to support your Preferred Strategy. Thus, you find it difficult to change because your goal for change and your Preferred Strategy are in conflict.

When you begin to understand the impact the Preferred Strategy has on you and the limitations on performance it creates, you must begin to reframe the strategy in a way that incorporates the change you are trying to make. In essence, you are creating an override program. The reframed strategy is not a replacement for the existing Preferred Strategy; it is an updated version with a wider range and scope that supplements or enhances the earlier version.

Take, for example, a Five who wants to improve in the emotional competency of communication but also believes that the best way to interact with the world is by Striving to be Detached (the Five's Preferred Strategy). To the Five the desire to remain detached is in conflict with the desire to improve communication, so the Five, even when becoming aware of her tendencies to not share her thoughts or feelings on an issue, will (consciously or not) resist changing.

In order for Fives to grow in this competency, they must reframe their Preferred Strategy in a way that resolves this conflict. They create an override program and tell themselves that healthy detachment—the ability to step back and objectively weigh all of the facts—depends on the ability to gather data through interaction with others.

A Six, who resists taking risks because it conflicts with his Preferred Strategy of Striving to be Secure, reframes his strategy to include the idea that taking appropriate risks at work will lead to success, thus ensuring his job security and avoiding the more serious insecurity that poor job performance would cause.

In short, you become authentic when you relentlessly and vigorously identify and resolve the conflict between your current worldview (or Preferred Strategy) and the change you wish to make. You resolve this conflict not by abandoning your strategy or changing your goal, but by expanding the way that you define the strategy so it can incorporate the change.

Phase Three: Take Action

Phase Three of The Awareness to Action Process is *Take Action*. Effective action is possible once authenticity is created and the conflict between your habitual Preferred Strategy and your goal for change is resolved.

This is where you begin to take those action steps that, deep down, you knew all along you should be taking. You identify specific behaviors that you wish to substitute for your less-effective behaviors. You create a specific action plan that you monitor and hold yourself accountable to, sometimes with the help of other people. It is only by creating and following the action plan that the new behaviors become rooted into the hard wiring of your brain and the reframed and expanded strategy becomes fixed.

You may object that you have tried making these changes before, with little effect. After all, who hasn't made a New Year's resolution, only to find himself falling back into the same behavior before January is through? The action steps found in each chapter are not revolutionary, but taking action is essential to change. *The key to creating lasting change, the key to The Awareness to Action Process, is in the interplay of all three steps*. When you understand the impact of the strategies and begin to expand the way you think about these strategies so they can include the changes you are trying to make, you will see change that lasts.

While the approach to performance improvement in this book (improving in the emotional competencies by understanding the impact of personality type and following The Awareness to Action Process) focuses on work situations, it is applicable to areas outside of work. The authors have taught this system to executives and managers, sales teams and self-help groups. Improving in the 16 emotional competencies will make you a better parent, spouse, little league coach, etc. In fact, there are few endeavors or interactions that will not be enhanced by following The Awareness to Action Process and improving emotional intelligence.

CHAPTER THREE

IDENTIFYING YOUR PERSONALITY TYPE

The life that is not examined is not worth living.
PLATO

Completing the Enneagram Personality Profile

The Enneagram Personality Profile will help you identify your personality type. This is accomplished by reading statements that are specific to each type and indicating which ones describe you best. Follow these instructions carefully, making sure to complete the statements before you read the *Descriptions of the Types*.

1. When responding to the statements, consider the kind of person you have been for most of your life. Most people believe that they are very different than when they were teenagers or in their early twenties. People also tend to change in a variety of ways as they mature. The Enneagram Personality Profile is most accurate when it reflects the characteristics that you have demonstrated during the majority of your life.

2. Estimate how much each statement reflects your personality on a scale from 1, which indicates you are *almost never* that way, to 5, which indicates that you are *almost always* that way.

3. Add the numbers and write the total in the space labeled Total Score at the bottom left of each page.

4. After completing the statements, follow the Scoring Instructions at the end of the Profile.

The authors recommend that you use this assessment only as a guide, not as the final authority on your type. The Enneagram Personality Profile is meant to help you narrow your choices so you can focus your observation and inquiry. Having a thorough knowledge of all the strategies, and inquiring into the motivation behind your behavior will help to make sure that you have correctly identified your type. See Appendix D for a further discussion on identifying type.

PERSONALITY TYPE A

Score the statements according to how true or applicable they are to you.

1	2	3	4	5
Almost Never	Rarely	Sometimes	Frequently	Almost Always

_____ Creative and have an artistic view of life.

_____ Feel different from others, as if "on the outside looking in."

_____ Tend to experience more melancholy than most people I know.

_____ Tend to be overly sensitive.

_____ Feel that something is missing in my life.

_____ Feel envious of other people's relationships, life styles, and accomplishments.

_____ Thrive in environments where I can express my creativity.

_____ When misunderstood, I can become withdrawn, self-conscious, and/or rebellious.

_____ Tend to be romantic and long for the great love of my life to come along.

_____ Can be caught in a fantasy world of romance and imagination.

_____ Enjoy having elegant, refined, unique things that no one else has.

_____ Attracted to what is intense and out of the ordinary.

_____ Tend to be moody, withdrawn, and self-absorbed when stressed.

_____ Tend to be compassionate, expressive, and supportive when not stressed.

_____ Can be deeply hurt by the slightest criticism.

_____ Tend to be reflective and to search for the meaning of my life.

_____ I strive to be unique and have done things to avoid being ordinary.

_____ Manners and good taste are extremely important to me.

_____ People have seen me as overly dramatic.

_____ Believe it is important to understand my own and other people's feelings.

Total Score_____

PERSONALITY TYPE B

Score the statements according to how true or applicable they are to you.

1	2	3	4	5
Almost Never	Rarely	Sometimes	Frequently	Almost Always

_____   Have a strong sense of responsibility and am a hard worker.

_____   Try to prepare for every contingency.

_____   Suspicious of others, and wonder about their motives.

_____   Making decisions on my own may cause me anxiety.

Safety and security are priorities in my life.

_____   Doubt my own decisions and opinions about myself.

_____   Believe it is important for people to be with other people or to belong to a group or an organization.

_____   Value the belief that everything is going to be all right, and yet, I often lack faith in this belief.

_____   Friends and family provide the support I feel is necessary in life.

_____   Tend to take things too seriously and to over-react to small issues.

_____   Don't really trust anybody I haven't known for a long time.

_____   Look for danger, unsafe people, or unsafe situations.

Tend to be suspicious, anxious, and defensive when stressed.

_____   Tend to be caring, warm, and loyal when not stressed.

_____   When feeling anxious I can be overly vigilant and controlling.

_____   When feeling relaxed I tend to be friendly and responsive to people.

_____   In a relationship, it has been difficult for me to trust the commitment of the other person.

_____   When afraid of something, I've done what was necessary to overcome my fear.

_____   Tend to worry more than other people.

_____   Motivated by the need to acquire security and social support.

Total Score _____

PERSONALITY TYPE C

Score the statements according to how true or applicable they are to you.

1	2	3	4	5
Almost Never	Rarely	Sometimes	Frequently	Almost Always

_____   Dislike confrontation and try to keep the peace.

_____   Easy going, "laid back," and optimistic.

_____   Listen patiently and can be very understanding and comforting to friends.

_____   Tend to procrastinate and to ignore or brush problems under the rug.

_____   Attracted to habits and routines, can relax easily and tune out reality through TV, daydreaming, a good book, etc.

_____   Have difficulty making decisions because "everything looks good."

_____   Routine and structure help me stay focused and accomplish things.

_____   Can be forgetful, neglectful, and "fuzzy" about details.

_____   Can feel angry even though I might look peaceful.

_____   Get tired easily and would love to take time during the day to relax and renew my energy.

_____   Can be a "homebody," and I enjoy the comfort and peace of home.

_____   In relationships, I seek harmony and peace through a sense of belonging, and/or by bonding with the other person.

_____   Dislike people nagging me; this makes me quite stubborn.

_____   May do routine and unimportant things before I tackle an important job.

_____   Tend to be withdrawn, forgetful, stubborn, and passive-aggressive when stressed.

_____   Tend to be open-minded, receptive, and very patient when not stressed.

_____   Tend to go along with what people say just to get them off my back.

_____   Too much to do or too many decisions to make can make me angry, anxious and/or depressed.

_____   Am told I'm a "nice guy" and dislike putting myself first.

_____   Motivated by the need to maintain peace of mind and harmony in my life.

Total Score

PERSONALITY TYPE D

Score the statements according to how true or applicable they are to you.

1	2	3	4	5
Almost Never	Rarely	Sometimes	Frequently	Almost Always

_____ Tend to be more emotional than most people I know.

_____ Consider relationships the most important part of my life.

_____ See myself as caring and helpful, and like to make people feel special and loved.

_____ Have trouble saying "no" to requests.

_____ Giving feels more comfortable then receiving.

_____ Need to feel close to people, and feel rejected and hurt if I don't experience that closeness.

_____ Like feeling indispensable and helping others become successful.

_____ Like to be gracious, outgoing, and connected with people.

_____ Avoid expressing negative feelings and like to compliment and flatter people.

_____ Have a strong need to be noticed, liked and appreciated for what I do for others.

_____ Like people to depend on me and to deliver on my promises.

_____ In intimate relationships, I value being told that I'm loved and wanted.

_____ People feel comfortable telling me their problems.

_____ Work very hard at maintaining relationships.

_____ Tend to be possessive and demanding when stressed.

_____ Tend to be loving, caring and supportive when not stressed.

_____ Know how to get people to like me.

_____ Can act like a martyr when not appreciated.

_____ Believe that my motives for helping others are noble and helpful.

_____ Motivated by the need to be appreciated, loved, and connected to people.

Total Score _____

PERSONALITY TYPE E

Score the statements according to how true or applicable they are to you.

1	2	3	4	5
Almost Never	Rarely	Sometimes	Frequently	Almost Always

_____   Good at marketing and selling myself and my ideas.

_____   Like doing more than one or two things at a time; enjoy "multi-tasking."

_____   Want to be "Number One," and am confident in my abilities.

_____   Love to work and be productive, and work has tended to be a top priority in my life.

_____   Have been goal-oriented for as long as I can remember.

_____   Value looking good, presenting a good first impression, and "dressing for success."

_____   Getting a product to market before the competition is more important than holding it back until it is "perfect."

_____   Prefer being with people more than being alone.

_____   Value finding the most practical, effective way to do a job.

_____   To impress, I may take on too much and make promises I can't keep.

_____   Have been told I am not in touch with my emotions.

_____   Believe that competition is a good thing, and tend to be very competitive.

_____   Value exceeding standards, and rising to the top of my profession.

_____   Tend to "spin" the facts, and be overly self-promoting when stressed.

_____   Tend to be honest, competent, and charming when not stressed.

_____   Believe that negative feelings are an obstacle to getting the job done.

_____   Find it easy to adapt to different people and situations.

_____   Enjoy supporting the careers of people I care about and who deserve it.

_____   Have difficulty understanding why people settle for second best.

_____   Motivated by being outstanding and being recognized for my personal success and achievements.

Total Score _____

PERSONALITY TYPE F

Score the statements according to how true or applicable they are to you.

1	2	3	4	5
Almost Never	Rarely	Sometimes	Frequently	Almost Always

_____ Uncomfortable around loud, emotional people.

_____ Enjoy analyzing things, gathering data and figuring out what makes things tick.

_____ Tend to be shy and withdrawn especially at social events.

_____ Tend to be more comfortable expressing ideas than emotions, especially spontaneously.

_____ May hesitate while I try to organize my thoughts, and may not speak at all if I'm not comfortable with what I want to say.

_____ I try to avoid confrontations.

_____ Enjoy spending time alone pursuing my personal interests.

_____ Sensitive to criticism, but try to hide that sensitivity.

_____ Enjoy the sense of independence that comes from living frugally.

_____ Prefer people not to know how I feel or what I think unless I tell them.

_____ People may find it difficult to follow my train of thought.

_____ Enjoy having control of my own time and private space.

_____ Easily annoyed by people who act unintelligent or uninformed.

_____ Have ideas, theories and opinions about almost everything.

_____ Tend to socialize with people who are interested in the same things as me.

_____ Tend to be distant, stubborn, and pessimistic when stressed.

_____ Tend to be insightful, objective, and sensitive when not stressed.

_____ Can be critical, cynical, argumentative, and can act intellectually superior.

_____ Don't mind working alone, and enjoy being self-sufficient.

_____ Rely on facts rather than emotions to make decisions.

Total Score _____

PERSONALITY TYPE G

Score the statements according to how true or applicable they are to you.

1	2	3	4	5
Almost Never	Rarely	Sometimes	Frequently	Almost Always

_____ Feel that life is to be enjoyed, and I'm optimistic about the future.

_____ Talkative, playful, and at times uninhibited.

_____ Like to leave my options open; "don't hem me in" describes me well.

_____ Have lots of friends and acquaintances and support them by cheering them up.

_____ Need to feel stimulated and like new, fun, exciting and different things.

_____ Tend to be idealistic and ambitious and want to contribute something positive to the world.

_____ I like to entertain and enjoy telling stories and getting laughs.

_____ Like to be "on the go," and may appear hyperactive to people.

_____ Enjoy trying many things and can do many different things fairly well.

_____ Hate to be bored, and I avoid doing boring, mundane things.

_____ Tend to do things in excess and to always want more.

_____ I'm super sensitive to possessive people; they make me feel uncomfortable.

_____ Have acted inappropriately, undisciplined, and/or rebellious when stressed..

_____ Tend to be fun-loving, imaginative, and optimistic when not stressed.

_____ When I find work that I like I can be very productive and enthusiastic.

_____ See no value in enduring suffering and pain, and I try to avoid it.

_____ Become frustrated if there is not enough time to do all the fun things I want to do.

_____ Dislike being around pessimistic, negative people.

_____ Tend to be excited and impatient about accomplishing plans.

_____ Motivated to feel excited, satisfied, happy and to do and experience more.

Total Score _____

PERSONALITY TYPE H

Score the statements according to how true or applicable they are to you.

1	2	3	4	5
Almost Never	Rarely	Sometimes	Frequently	Almost Always

_____ Stand up for what I want and need in life.

_____ People see me as courageous and look to me as a natural leader.

_____ Value strength and autonomy, take pride in taking care of my own needs, and expect others to do the same for themselves.

_____ Impatient with people who are indirect or indecisive.

_____ I am assertive and like to compete and win.

_____ I am extremely protective of my loved owns and feel good about helping the underdog.

_____ Like expressing my power and being the boss and/or being in charge.

_____ I am not gullible: you must earn my trust and I will challenge your loyalty.

_____ Like taking risks and the excitement of competition.

_____ Work hard and know how to get things done.

_____ Love to be challenged and enjoy a good fight.

_____ Would rather be respected than liked.

_____ Feel I must take charge because I am the strongest and most decisive person in the group.

_____ Proud about being direct, telling it "like it is," and expressing "tough love."

_____ Tend to be rebellious, controlling, and insensitive when stressed.

_____ Tend to be energetic, self-confident, and helpful when not stressed.

_____ Am uncomfortable expressing emotions other than anger.

_____ When I trust people, I can let down my guard and be more sensitive.

_____ Tend to go overboard in the pursuit of fun and pleasure.

_____ Motivated by the need to protect myself and my loved ones, and to be powerful and in control of my life.

Total Score _____

PERSONALITY TYPE I

Score the statements according to how true or applicable they are to you.

1	2	3	4	5
Almost Never	Rarely	Sometimes	Frequently	Almost Always

_____ Have a strong sense of right and wrong and strive for perfection.

_____ Take pride in being self-disciplined, moderate and fair.

_____ Personal integrity is extremely important to me.

_____ Tend to be more logical than emotional.

_____ Can be too serious and lack spontaneity.

_____ Critical of myself (my own worst critic) and find it easy to be judgmental and critical of other people as well.

_____ Easily discern what is wrong in a situation and how it could be done better.

_____ Tend to be a workaholic and a perfectionist.

_____ Value being well organized and punctuality in myself and others.

_____ Morals and ethics are more important than compassion and tolerance.

_____ Tend to see the glass as "half empty" and to look for what needs fixing.

_____ Do not consider being a perfectionist a negative thing, and like to make sure all the details are just right.

_____ Tend to be intolerant, inflexible, and demanding when stressed.

_____ Tend to be rational, reasonable, and accepting when not stressed.

_____ Fear being criticized or judged as being improper by other people.

_____ Find it difficult to forgive and can carry a grudge for a long time.

_____ Have difficulty seeing the "gray" areas of an issue, and tend to see things in black and white.

_____ Have difficulty admitting I'm wrong.

_____ Believe that rules, regulations, policies and procedures have a purpose and should be followed—and am frustrated when others break rules.

_____ Motivated by the need to be correct, fair, and self-disciplined.

Total Score _____

Scoring Instructions

1. Transfer your scores from the Total Scores at the bottom of each page to the appropriate lines below. For example, the score from *Personality Type A* should be recorded on the line directly below A. The numbers beneath the lines on this page correspond to the Enneagram personality types. Your highest score usually, but not always, indicates your type.

	A	B	C	D	E	F	G	H	I
Score	___	___	___	___	___	___	___	___	___
Corresponding Type	4	6	9	2	3	5	7	8	1

2. Enter your three highest scores and their corresponding type in the appropriate boxes below.

First Highest	Type

Second Highest	Type

Third Highest	Type

3. Record the type from question 2 above (either 4, 6, 9, 2, 3, 5, 7, 8, or 1) associated with your First Highest Score.

4. Now read the *Descriptions of the Types* beginning on the next page. Which type description best fits you?

5. If questions 3 and 4 above do not agree, what is your best estimation of your personality type?

DESCRIPTIONS OF THE TYPES

Ones: Ones interact with the world by Striving to be Perfect. They are often models of decorum, clear logic, and appropriate behavior. They focus on rules, procedures, and making sure that they are always doing the "right thing." When they overdo their Striving to be Perfect they can become critical, judgmental, and unwilling to take risks. Under stress, Ones may fear that if they have too much fun they will become irresponsible.

Twos: Twos interact with the world by Striving to be Connected. They are often selfless, caring, and nurturing. They focus on helping others meet their needs; they build rapport easily and enjoy finding a common bond with others. When they overdo their Striving to be Connected they may fail to take care of their own needs and end up becoming emotionally dependent on others. Under stress, Twos may fear that if they are not closely connected to others they will become isolated.

Threes: Threes interact with the world by Striving to be Outstanding. They work hard to exceed standards and to be successful in whatever they undertake. They place high value on productivity and presenting an image of being a winner in whatever environment they are in. When they overdo their Striving to be Outstanding they may become attention seeking and may value image over substance. When stressed, Threes may fear that if they are not making great efforts to be excellent they will become mediocre.

Fours: Fours interact with the world by Striving to be Unique. They generally approach their lives creatively, in fresh and interesting ways. They gravitate toward things and experiences that are elegant, refined, or unusual. When they overdo their Striving to be Unique they may feel misunderstood, and they may withdraw from others and become isolated. When stressed, Fours may fear that if they do not put their own special touch on their world and their experiences their individuality will become repressed.

Fives: Fives interact with the world by Striving to be Detached. They are observant, logical, and generally reserved. They focus on problem solving, innovative ideas, and data gathering. When they overdo their Striving to be Detached they can end up being dull—out of touch with their experiences and emotions. When stressed, Fives may fear that if they do not remain detached and guarded they will become uncontrolled.

Sixes: Sixes interact with the world by Striving to be Secure. They find security in being part of something bigger than themselves, such as a group or tradition. They are careful, responsible, and protective of the welfare of the group. They focus on maintaining consistency, tradition, and cohesion. When they overdo their Striving to be Secure they may fail to take the risks necessary for high performance and settle for mediocrity. When stressed, Sixes may fear that if they relax their guard they will be vulnerable to possible dangers.

Sevens: Sevens interact with the world by Striving to be Excited. They are upbeat, enthusiastic, optimistic, and curious. They focus on possibilities and options and keeping others entertained. When they overdo their Striving to be Excited they may fail to follow through, become easily distracted, and act irresponsibly. When stressed, Sevens may fear that if they do not keep options open they will miss out on something.

Eights: Eights interact with the world by Striving to be Powerful. They are action-oriented self-starters who love to be in charge. They focus on getting things done and overcoming obstacles that may lie in their way. When they overdo their Striving to be Powerful they may not adhere to the rules or norms that others expect them to follow and their behavior can become uncontrolled. When stressed, Eights may fear that if they become too connected to others or experience their own emotions too deeply they will become dependent on others.

Nines: Nines interact with the world by Striving to be Peaceful. They are calm, pleasant, and likable. They focus on maintaining a sense of inner harmony by minimizing their own needs and concentrating on the needs of others. When they overdo their Striving to be Peaceful they can become passive, relying on others to make decisions for them. When stressed, Nines may fear that if they place too much importance on themselves they will be seen as attention seeking.

CHAPTER FOUR

TYPE ONE: *STRIVING TO BE PERFECT*

Man, being incomplete, is not at rest and is therefore always striving
for his completion. And this itself is his perfection.
JUDAH LOW

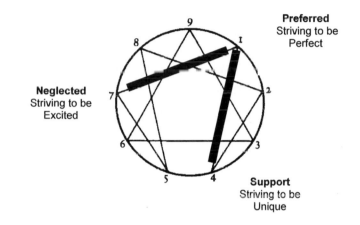

Portrait of a One

Peter is the director of compliance for a financial planning company.
He takes pride in his knowledge of the industry, his skill at creating a
smoothly running department, and his ability to minimize mistakes.
Peter had worked in the operations department before he was
promoted to director of compliance. He felt he had inherited a major
challenge. As he put it, "Compliance was a mess and needed fixing."
His first day on the job he called a meeting of his staff, introduced
himself, and announced his goals: "I intend to put this department in
order," he said, "to discover mistakes and correct them because
mistakes are something I can't tolerate." His staff listened quietly and
attentively. "Carelessness has no place in this department," he added.

He talked about his experience at his previous position and how
he had increased efficiency by installing a system that discovered
mistakes so early in processing that no customer ever saw them.
"Hard work and attention to detail are what I value and what I
reward," he said. He told his people that he would be spending his
first few weeks on the job examining "with a fine-tooth comb" the
existing system and people's work practices for inefficiencies and

inaccuracies, and that he would be asking each of them for recommendations on how to improve things.

That was three years ago. His staff has gone from eight to five people, and Peter likes it that way. He feels that the people he has now are more focused on quality and efficiency. "There's much less nonsense now," he says. "People know their jobs and we get things done correctly. We don't mind audits now because we follow the regulations to the letter."

He is most valued for his knowledge of compliance standards, his consistency and work ethic, and his dedication to doing things correctly. The most frequently heard complaint about Peter is that he is inflexible, uncreative, and not a people person. People see him as too "by the book." He tends to have a negative view, preferring to concentrate on what is wrong rather than what is right. He watches his employees vigilantly, micromanages them, and tends to be stingy when evaluating them in performance reviews, rarely handing out praise. He has an image of the ideal employee and judges himself and his people by this ideal. "No one is perfect. No one deserves an A," he is known to say.

Peter is a One. Of course, not all Ones have exactly the same traits as Peter does, but some of his characteristics will resonate with you if you are a One. You may also recognize some of these behaviors if you know a One. Peter, like all Ones, is motivated by striving to be perfect.

The rest of this chapter explores the personality dynamics of Ones and shows how they can improve performance in the emotional competencies.

The Strategies

The Preferred Strategy: Striving to be Perfect

Ones interact with the world by Striving to be Perfect. Different Ones may use different words for "Striving to be Perfect," such as wanting to be correct, right, proper, logical, rigorous, etc. Regardless of the words they use, however, Ones are often models of decorum, clear logic, and appropriate behavior. They focus on rules, procedures and making sure that they are always doing the "right thing."

When Ones overdo their Preferred Strategy, "perfect" becomes distorted into "repressed." Stressed Ones deal with the world by becoming rigid, judgmental, and critical of themselves and others. Their fear of making a mistake may make it difficult for them to take decisive action.

The Neglected Strategy: Striving to be Excited

The strategy at Point Seven, Striving to be Excited, in some ways contradicts the One's desire to be perfect. Excitement, to the One, implies heightened emotion and spontaneity, two things that can lead to errors in judgment or execution. Therefore, Ones become uncomfortable with this strategy and "neglect" it. Rather than seeing the full value of Striving to be Excited, they distort it and see it as *irresponsibility*. They may fear that if they have too much fun, show their emotions, or become light-hearted they will make mistakes and become irresponsible.

This is not to say that Ones are always stern and humorless or incapable of showing emotion or having fun. In fact, most Ones have a wry sense of humor and devilish streak. However, their humor is usually understated and sometimes focused on sarcasm; even at their most light-hearted they seem to be holding onto the reins, keeping themselves from going too far and letting their guard down.

The Contradiction: Restraint vs. Indulgence

The neglect of the natural and healthy desire to express their feelings and act with excitement causes Ones to act out the Neglected Strategy in subtle and predictable ways. Ones usually act with restraint, but sometimes they act in indulgent ways. For example, they may secretly overeat or pursue other pleasures while being wracked with guilt.

When Ones become aware that they are acting this way they will quickly revert to their typical "One-ish" behavior of being proper, discreet, and "well-behaved."

The Support Strategy: Striving to be Unique

Ones use Striving to be Unique to reinforce being perfect. They are comfortable in the role of moral authority and are unafraid to be the lone voice standing up for what they think is right. Ones are autonomous and not easily swayed by the demands of the crowd, often refusing to jump on the bandwagon of public opinion. However, under stress they may try to force their unique interpretation of what is right onto others and then begin to feel alienated and depressed when others disagree with them. They begin to lose objectivity, forgetting that their opinion is one of many possible opinions of what is "right."

Ones at Their Best

When Ones are at their best they use all three strategies naturally and appropriately rather than in the habitual patterns described above. They are rigorous and detail-oriented without being perfectionistic and critical; they are lighthearted and display their emotions without overindulging; and they stand up for what they believe is right without losing objectivity and ignoring other points of view.

Ones At a Glance

Examples of Ones: Ralph Nader, Pope John Paul II, Martha Stewart, Jimmy Carter, Margaret Thatcher, Sandra Day O'Connor, George Will.

Chief Asset: *Precision.* Ones are precise and methodical in their approach to life. They have an ability to make clear, logical decisions about appropriate action and behavior.

What They Like in Others: Competence, high quality, adherence to principles and procedures.

What They Dislike in Others: Emotionality, illogical behavior, rule breaking.

How They Frustrate Others: Perfectionism, pessimism, rigidity, judging.

Approach to Problem Solving: "We need to be logical about this and do the correct thing."

Belief About Work: "Things work best when everyone follows the rules."

How Others See Ones: Rational, proper, conscientious, disciplined, and discerning, but sometimes rigid, critical, condescending, humorless, and remote.

Ones Get Into Trouble When They Tell Themselves: "I know how things *should* be. I can improve myself, my environment, and others to fit my ideals."

Blind Spot: *Criticism.* Ones are often unaware of their tendency to be critical and its affect on their relationships. They are on a mission to set the world straight. Their attempt to do so often comes across as criticism and nagging. Ones believe that they know how things should be and feel that they have an obligation to fix the flaws in their environment. They feel that they are only trying to be helpful and are often surprised when others interpret their comments as criticism.

The One Leader: The Administrator

The High Side of the Administrator: Ones create order and clarity, and they institute and enforce policies and procedures.

The Low Side of the Administrator: Ones can be rigid, inflexible, remote, and uninspiring and may focus on what is wrong rather than what is right.

Where They Shine: *Setting and following procedures.* Ones are great in roles that require consistency of method and logic.

The Enneagram Emotional Competencies

As we have already discussed in Chapter Two, *emotional intelligence* is the ability to (1) identify your emotions and manage your responses to them, and (2) identify the emotions of others and manage your responses to them. The following *emotional competencies* are a set of sixteen specific capabilities based on emotional intelligence. They indicate how well Ones use emotional intelligence personally and socially.

PERSONAL COMPETENCIES

Self-Awareness

Self-Awareness: ability to identify one's thought processes, emotions, and skills
Typically: Ones are more adept at identifying their thought processes and skills than their emotions. They feel compelled to be rational and correct, so they tend to focus on how sensible and logical their thinking process is. Ones often find emotions to be illogical and distracting. In particular, Ones are often unaware of their anger because they label it as frustration rather than seeing it for what it is: anger.
When Stressed: Ones' inner critics tend to cloud their assessment of their skills, and they may become overly critical of their abilities because they evaluate themselves by unrealistically high standards. Stress causes Ones to grow increasingly angry, though they may feel guilt for being angry and deny the emotion. This causes them to lose touch with what they are genuinely experiencing, and reduces self-awareness.

Self-Confidence: confidence in one's powers and abilities
Typically: Ones are hardworking and driven to meet high standards, so their history of accomplishment gives them some degree of self-confidence in their ability to get things done. Their desire to fix the world compels them to take an active, assertive stance. They are also confident that they know better than others what to do, but at times Ones can worry about making mistakes in implementation. They may seem self-assured and often find themselves in leadership roles, telling others what to do and how best to do it.

When Stressed: There is an underlying insecurity in Ones that starts to show itself under stress. Ones fear being seen as flawed yet they have a tendency to see and perhaps even obsess over all of their own shortcomings. This can seriously undermine their self-confidence, making them feel inadequate and unsure of their judgment and abilities. This insecurity may make them overcompensate, and they can become aggressive and angry in their opinions and attitudes.

Self-Management

Self-Control: restraint exercised over one's impulses, emotions or desires
Typically. Ones shine in this competency. Their personality is structured around this very issue—controlling their impulses, emotions and desires. They fear being imperfect and are proud of their ability to practice discipline. Ones often use this quality to great benefit to themselves and others, serving as dependable, focused and hardworking employees, and as sober and discerning advisors or mentors. They use self-control as a way to avoid being sidetracked by emotional reactions, either their own or those of others.
When Stressed: Ones may become too self-controlled, becoming emotionless and distant. In an effort to maintain control, they start trying to control others. They may become demanding, impatient and critical, projecting their own sense of imperfection onto others. They tend to pressure themselves and those around them to work harder and strive for improvement.

Adaptability: flexibility in handling change
Typically: Ones have very strong and often fixed opinions on the way things should be, so they may have difficulty when others want to make changes. They are usually vocal with their opinions, and their resistance to change may at times make them seem uncooperative and pessimistic. In particular, they find it difficult to change their morals, standards, and values, which they see as nonnegotiable. At the same time, they are constantly seeking to improve both themselves and their world, so they are often pushing for some kind of change. As with many other types, Ones' ability to adapt will be greatly affected by how much control they feel they have over the change and how closely the change corresponds to the way they think things should be.
When Stressed: Ones become more rigid in their opinions and ideas and work hard to resist change. They develop a "right is right and

wrong is wrong" attitude and may begin applying it to policies and procedures. Their fear of making mistakes grows, and they become more conservative, clinging to the tried and true rather than taking the risk of trying something new and possibly failing. They lose faith in others' judgment and ability to make good decisions about new ways of doing things.

Trustworthiness: maintaining standards of honesty and integrity
Typically: Ones are often ethical beacons and take pride in maintaining high standards. They are dependable and reliable and often can be counted on to perform to higher standards than are expected from others. Ones are careful about the promises they make, and they stick to their word and expect others to do the same. Ones use their ability to be in touch with their high standards to be fair in their assessments and evaluations of others, and as bosses they usually do not play favorites among their employees.
When Stressed: Ones may go into denial or change the subject rather than admit when they are wrong or cheating on their own standards. For example, if they see themselves as a healthy eater, they may hide candy bars in their desk drawer. In their drive to be correct, Ones may also focus more on rules than on ethics. They can become rigid in enforcing laws and procedures, even when exceptions are clearly justified. Very stressed Ones may exempt themselves from the rules but demand that others follow them.

Optimism: ability to anticipate and expect the best possible outcome
Typically: Ones struggle with this competency and tend to see the glass as half empty. They see the world as imperfect and needing improvement, so they focus on fixing it. Their fear of making mistakes causes Ones to prepare for what could go wrong rather than what could go right. This focus makes it easy to overlook positive possibilities. Ones are great believers in Murphy's Law—that what *can* go wrong *will* go wrong—and they often do not trust others to do things correctly.
When Stressed: Ones become even more pessimistic and doubtful about the future. They feel that it is their responsibility to fix a broken world, but they innately doubt their capacity to correct all that needs to be corrected. Stressed Ones focus more and more on the negative, becoming fatalistic and doubting that anyone is up to fixing things.

Initiative: readiness to act on opportunities
Typically: Ones tend to be careful and conservative, not readily willing to take risks. Their fear of making mistakes may cause them

to delay a decision rather than risk making the wrong choice. They often see others as reckless and themselves as the voice of reason whose responsibility it is to ensure that no one else acts too quickly. While they may struggle with spontaneity and taking risks, they are usually proactive when it comes to righting a wrong or improving a process.

When Stressed: Ones' fear of making mistakes grows, and they can become more indecisive. After a period of indecisiveness their inner criticism may force them to finally make a decision that is hasty and poorly reasoned. The end result could be that they make mistakes, which is exactly what they feared in the first place.

Achievement Drive: striving to meet or improve a standard of excellence

Typically: Ones hold themselves to very high standards of excellence. Their drive to be flawless makes them want to do better and improve their own performance and that of the group. "Good enough" is often *not* good enough for Ones. They feel the need to be perfect, or to at least attain a higher standard than those around them. Achievement helps Ones let their relentless inner critic temporarily rest. In addition to their inner drive to succeed, Ones see achievement as a way to prove their merit and to gain rewards and recognition for a job well done. Ones focus far more on achievement as the path to success than on such things as relationships, political correctness, likeability, charisma and connections.

When Stressed: Initially, stress may make Ones work even harder to achieve. They may feel that the only way to be sure they are doing the right thing is to work much harder and do a better job than everyone else. However, their tendency to doubt themselves may interfere with their desire to strive to improve standards of excellence. Again, fear of making a mistake or being found wanting makes stressed Ones cautious and hesitant. They may also tend to turn their attention outward onto others and they go from trying to improve themselves to trying to fix others. They may also blame others for hindering their productivity and efficiency.

Resiliency: capacity to endure in the face of obstacles

Typically: Obstacles provide Ones with a verification of their belief that the world is imperfect, and they believe that obstacles are part of the natural course of life. They believe that part of being "good" involves working hard in the face of obstacles. Because they tend to be somewhat pessimistic, Ones seem to expect roadblocks and are therefore prepared for them when they arrive. This preparation makes it possible for them to continue functioning when others may be set back.

When Stressed: Ones can become very stubborn, a negative form of resilience. They can see themselves as martyrs, believing that life is not meant to be fun. They may seem to view the ability to endure in the face of life's struggles as a gift and carry their suffering like a badge of their righteousness. They may also blame themselves and others for setbacks.

SOCIAL COMPETENCIES

Attunement to Others

Empathy: awareness of and participation in others' feelings, ideas, and needs
Typically: Ones generally work to suppress their emotions and focus on logic. Therefore, they are not inclined to be highly attuned to the emotional states of others. Ones also have a tendency to believe that they are right and may have difficulty empathizing with others' ideas when those ideas conflict with their own. If Ones see the needs of others as "legitimate," they are good at meeting them; doing so helps them reinforce their image of being good, righting wrongs, and reforming the world.

When Stressed: Ones tend to struggle with empathy. They become more self-critical and project their own needs onto other people. They criticize in people what they refuse to acknowledge in themselves—shortcomings and emotional needs. Stressed Ones expect people to be stoic and focus on work rather than emotion.

Political Awareness: reading a group's emotional currents and power relationships
Typically: Ones are not as astute at reading emotional currents as they are at reading power relationships. Because they are highly influenced by their inner critic—they are accustomed to listening to an authority figure in their minds—they are attuned to authority figures and sources of power. Ones are sometimes uncomfortable with authority figures because they may expect to be judged by them. Ones work hard to repress their emotions and often feel that emotions are inappropriate in the workplace. This means that they often overlook others' emotions and may not see the impact that emotions can have on relationships.

When Stressed: Ones often resent the political process because of what they see as the compromises and deception involved in gaining political power. They feel that people should be judged on their merits, rather than on political skills. They pay even less attention to emotions and may become frustrated by authorities who do not meet the One's high standards of achievement and ethical behavior.

Communication: listening openly and sending convincing messages
Typically: Ones tend to be highly opinionated and may struggle with listening openly and without judgment. They value objectivity and tend to have a "just-the-facts" approach, which often makes them miss the nonverbal elements that are critical components of communication. They sometimes struggle in listening to others without offering feedback or advice. When sending messages, Ones are usually logical, thorough, and earnest rather than passionate and inspiring. They instill trust in their listeners through their focus on what is correct and rational.

When Stressed: Ones struggle with being open to other points of view, and their messages may be peppered with advice and criticism. Their communication becomes controlled by their own rigidly held opinions rather than the facts, and listeners may feel unheard and invalidated. They may try to convince others by instilling guilt or appealing
to an arbitrary higher authority rather than objective logic.

Relationship Building

Leadership: inspiring and leading individuals and groups
Typically: Ones are often ambitious and driven to become leaders because they believe that they know the right thing to do. They have great clarity and vision, and they can focus on the important issues without being distracted. They are motivated by high ethical principles and lead for moral reasons rather than by what polls say, or for sheer love of power or attention. Because of their high integrity and certainty, followers usually trust Ones and believe that they will be steered in the right direction and not taken advantage of. Highly aware Ones are sure of themselves, speak with clarity, strength, directness and moral certitude. What is often missing in their leadership is an appeal to people's emotions.

When Stressed: Ones can become rigid, critical and demanding of their followers or subordinates. Their lack of emotion can also make it difficult for people to feel close to them, further undermining their ability to lead. They may drive themselves too hard, making them seem unapproachable and distant, and they may also drive their employees to overwork. They may aim toward a lofty vision but focus more on the consequences of failure than the rewards of achievement.

Cooperation: *working with others toward shared goals*
Typically: Ones are cooperative if they believe in the correctness and logic of the group's goals. It is important to them to be seen as contributors and team players. However, if they do not believe that the goals are the correct ones for them or the organization, they will be uncooperative or will cooperate grudgingly. They may try to do everything themselves, believing that no one else can do the job as thoroughly as they will.
When Stressed: Ones may have difficulty working with others. They can become more rigid and standoffish and if they do not agree with the goals espoused by the group they may even challenge the group and argue about goals. Stressed Ones prefer to work on their own so they do not have to put up with the shortcomings and personal foibles of others.

Influence: *wielding effective tactics for persuasion*
Typically: To the degree that they balance their factual, logical, principled presentation with the human side of an argument, Ones are effective at influencing others. They tend, however, to concentrate on being logical and factual. Charisma and personal appeal often influence people more than mere facts and data, so Ones may struggle in this competency. Ones often manage to find passion when they are trying to correct a social or moral wrong, and this is where they are at their most persuasive. Ones are well prepared, have great clarity and confidence in their opinions, so people tend to listen to them.
When Stressed: Ones can become dogmatic, demanding and insistent that others see things their way. They focus on criticizing rather than persuading. Rather than serving to influence others, this behavior may turn people away even when the One is correct.

Conflict Management: *negotiating and resolving disputes*
Typically: Ones are able to leave their own emotions aside, are logical and dispassionate, and generally do a good job at managing conflict. Self-aware Ones do not take disputes personally and will generally not dwell on problems once they have been resolved. However, Ones may have a tendency to see things in black and white and downplay the importance of emotions in negotiating and

resolving conflict. They tend to be logical in disputes, but their logic may be more geared to making their point than to listening to the logical arguments of others.

When Stressed: Ones can become rigid and entrenched in their own point of view: Black gets blacker and white gets whiter, and they may be unwilling to hear what the other is saying, especially if a moral or ethical point is in question. They become demanding that others see their logic and may lose their temper. As stress increases, Ones have a tendency to either become strident or to shut down, and they have difficulty staying dispassionately engaged in the dispute.

The Awareness to Action Process

Improving Optimism

Optimism is an area where many Ones struggle. Unlocking the One's full capacity for high performance often lies in improving in this competency. What follows is an example of how a One might work on this key developmental area; it is not a literal "cook book" for all Ones, and you may find that improving performance in other competencies is more critical for you. The purpose of this example is to demonstrate how you might use the three steps of The Awareness to Action Process to identify *your* specific developmental areas and improve in those areas.

Other competencies that Ones would do well to improve in are Adaptability and Empathy. Optimism, Adaptability, and Empathy are interrelated and improvement in one often facilitates improvement in the other two. Optimism, the ability to anticipate and expect the best possible outcome, can make it easier to adapt to change. Ones who are optimistic have learned to be more flexible and to be cooperative and less fearful about making mistakes. Empathy helps Ones to be open to and participate in the feelings of others, which helps them resist believing they are always right. Being optimistic and seeing the glass as "half full" helps Ones to adapt to change and be empathic.

When formulating your own action plan, work on one or two important goals at a time; create small steps that will move you toward each goal; go from easiest to most difficult, and celebrate your success.

Phase One: Build Awareness

Identify a goal.

- Improve performance in the emotional competency of Optimism.

Identify your current behaviors.

- "I tend to focus on what is wrong and what needs fixing. I usually don't trust other people to do things correctly. I am often fearful of making mistakes; this makes me prepare for what could go wrong rather than what could go right. I also tend to blame myself or others for setbacks rather than seeing them as normal, manageable events."

Phase Two: Develop Authenticity

Identify how your Preferred Strategy is in conflict with improving in this competency.

- "To me, Striving to be Perfect means fixing what is broken, and making things exactly right. This involves looking for what is *not* perfect, being on guard about what could go wrong, who's going to mess up next, and how I can fix things. I see people, organizations, and systems as flawed and in need of repair and I don't have much hope in human nature. All of these are in conflict with Optimism."

Revise your strategy so that it incorporates improvement in this competency. (Remember that when Ones overdo their Striving to be Perfect they can become repressed and fail to take the risks necessary for high performance.)

- "Harboring a negative attitude, micromanaging people, and being critical of myself and others undermines my efforts to be perfect. Being perfect means taking a broader view of people and things. Being perfect also involves seeing the best in myself and others rather than focusing on flaws. Mistakes are a part of life and are really opportunities to improve, to develop myself, and to help others become more effective."

Phase Three: Take Action

Devise and Execute an Action Plan; be sure that it involves a goal, action steps, a person who will help monitor your success, and a timeline for completion. See Appendix C for a sample Action Plan. Sample action steps are listed below.

- Stop torturing yourself and others about not being perfect. See setbacks as inevitable events in all aspects of life, and not caused by your personal shortcomings. Forgive yourself and others. Accept the fact that good can come from almost any mistake because you can always *learn* from your mistakes.

- Recognize the high cost you pay by focusing on the fear of failure rather than the anticipation of success. Concentrating on who's right and who's wrong rather than persisting in seeking your goals despite obstacles leads to emotional exhaustion, anger, frustration and burn out. See optimism as an important component of success, especially in stressful situations.

- Stop blaming and criticizing and start complimenting. Your blind spot—a quality that you don't see in yourself but that others do—is criticism. What you say may often be interpreted as critical, even when you don't see it that way. Remember that an encouraging word goes a long way in helping others improve.

- See Appendix B, General Recommendations for Growth.

CHAPTER FIVE

TYPE TWO:
STRIVING TO BE CONNECTED

*Only in relationships can you know yourself, not in abstraction,
and certainly not in isolation.*
J. KRISHNAMURTI

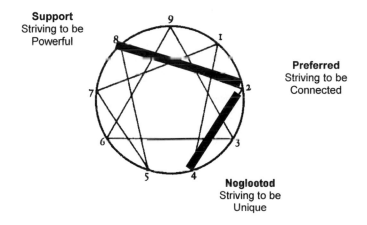

Support
Striving to be
Powerful

Preferred
Striving to be
Connected

Noglootod
Striving to be
Unique

Portrait of a Two

Mary manages the support staff for a not-for-profit, organ donor organization. Eleven administrative assistants report to her. She has an exceptional ability to understand the emotional needs of people, and never hesitates to supply support for her boss, clients, and her direct reports. She loves her job and is very close to the people in her office, especially the ones she supervises. She shares details of her home life with people in the office, and has little sense of separation between home and work. She likes to refer to her group as "one big, happy family—and I'm the Mom." She prides herself in being her people's greatest advocate. "My ongoing battle is to get my staff acknowledged for all that they do. I think they are the unsung heroes of this organization," She is a caring, supportive boss who is dedicated to the welfare of her people and to the work that the organization does.

She has worked for pharmaceutical, insurance, and manufacturing companies, but, as she puts it, "I found my home when I came here. I feel like I'm contributing directly to helping people.

What could be more rewarding than being part of an organization that helps save lives?"

Her direct reports see her in a variety of ways. "She's a sweet person, but she really gets emotional at times," one administrative assistant told us. "She constantly wants to know if I'm OK, if there's anything she can do to help me. She'll ask about my family, what I'm doing after work. To be honest, she can get too personal. I prefer to separate my personal life from my work life." As an afterthought, she added, "I feel bad saying anything negative about Mary; she really is an amazingly generous person. And she's helped me a lot."

Another employee added, "She's a caring person, and she wants to be your friend, but when the stress of this place gets to her she can get really demanding, expecting me to do things that aren't in my job description. I think she tries to make me feel guilty, telling me I should be glad that I work here and that I should look for ways to contribute more."

Mary reports to the director of Human Resources, who will tell you, "She's the most supportive person I've ever met, but I think she's too involved in the lives of her people and she takes everything personally," adding, "Mary feels that her group doesn't get praised enough—and of course that's a reflection on her, which means she isn't being acknowledged for the good, caring person she is." That's when the problems start. When Mary feels unappreciated, she becomes overly dependent on people, particularly her boss. "When Mary is feeling neglected, she's in my office every five minutes. She demands a lot of attention and handholding. When I tell her that I can't spend so much time with her, her reply is, 'I think I deserve a little attention after all I've done for this organization.' She'll complain that the CEO doesn't know the hours she puts in and all the things that her group does. In a nutshell, she's a hard working, supportive, employee, but when the tension mounts she becomes a bit needy."

Mary is a Two. Of course, not all Twos have exactly the same traits that Mary does, but some of her characteristics will resonate with you if you are a Two. You may also recognize some of these behaviors if you know a Two. Mary, like all Twos, is motivated by striving to be connected to people and to their own feelings.

The rest of this chapter explores the personality dynamics of Twos and shows how they can improve performance in the emotional competencies.

The Strategies

The Preferred Strategy: Striving to be Connected

Twos interact with the world by Striving to be Connected. Different Twos may use different words for "Striving to be Connected," such as wanting to be helpful, giving, close, appreciated, loved, etc. Regardless of the words they use, however, Twos are often selfless, caring, and nurturing. They focus on helping others meet their needs; they build rapport easily, and enjoy finding a common bond with others.

When Twos overdo their Preferred Strategy, "connection" becomes distorted into "dependence." Stressed Twos deal with the world by feeling that they must be intimately aligned with people they deem important. They have difficulty setting boundaries and they may fail to take care of their own needs, hoping that someone will do it for them.

The Neglected Strategy: Striving to be Unique

The strategy at Point Four, Striving to be Unique, in some ways contradicts the Two's desire to be connected. Uniqueness, to the Two, implies a willingness to stand alone, unsupported by the opinions or admiration of others. Therefore, Twos become uncomfortable with this strategy and "neglect" it. Rather than seeing the full value of Striving to be Unique, Twos distort it and see it as *isolation.* They may fear that if they are too "different" they will lose the positive regard of the people they want to connect with. They may also feel that being unique is selfish and uncaring and leads to being disconnected and alone.

This is not to say that Twos are incapable of being creative or independent. They are often found in artistic fields and they are often tenacious advocates for their point of view, even if it contrasts with others in authority. However, this advocacy is often in support of a relationship, such as protecting their families, co-workers, or subordinates rather than on their own behalf.

The Contradiction: Giving vs. Envy

The neglect of the natural and healthy desire to value yourself for your own benefit (an aspect of *uniqueness*) causes Twos to act out the

Neglected Strategy in subtle and predictable ways. Two's are usually giving, but are sometimes envious. For example, they may demand that people focus on them and their needs, and become jealous of the attention paid to others. When Twos become aware that they are acting this way they will quickly revert to their typical "Two-ish" behavior of being self-sacrificing and supportive.

The Support Strategy: Striving to be Powerful

Twos use Striving to be Powerful, the strategy found at Point Eight, to reinforce being connected. Twos' ability to use their influence to 'make things happen' ensures that people will like them, and helps them stay connected to others. They are protective and tireless advocates for the people they care about. However, under stress Twos may also become aggressive, domineering, or manipulative, acting as if they are forcing others to make a choice of either loving or hating them. They may be histrionic and coerce or bully others into making the changes the Two thinks they should make. Twos can also use this aggressiveness to resist making changes they don't want to make.

Twos At Their Best

When Twos are at their best they use all three strategies naturally and appropriately rather than in the habitual patterns described above. They have close, connected relationships without being clingy or dependent; they are able to get their own needs met without being jealous of the attention and consideration others receive; and they are independent and assertive without being volatile and manipulative.

Twos At a Glance

Examples of Twos: Sammy Davis, Jr., Florence Nightingale, Richard Simmons, Mother Teresa, Eleanor Roosevelt, James Lipton.

Chief Asset: *Connection.* Twos have a unique ability to understand and empathize with the needs of others. They can read emotional currents and provide just the thing that others need.

What They Like in Others: Friendliness, sharing of feelings, display of emotion.

What They Dislike in Others: Coldness, unavailability, lack of needs.

How They Frustrate Others: Flattery, emotionality, intrusiveness.

Approach to Problem Solving: "I'm fine; is there anything I can do to help *you*?"

Belief About Work: "Things work best when I can help people succeed."

How Others See Twos: Helpful, concerned, expressive, dependable, and engaging, but sometimes intrusive, angry, flattering, prideful, and manipulative.

Twos Get Into Trouble When They Tell Themselves: "People who really appreciate what I do for them are more important than others and deserve a larger share of my attention."

Blind Spot: *Demandingness.* Twos are often unaware of their tendency to be demanding and its affect on their relationships. Twos may act like a spoiled and pampered prince or princess and demand that they are appreciated. They exert pressure on others to meet their needs, but feel they deserve this special treatment because they do so much, and care so much, for others. They express their entitlement as, "That's what I would do for you."

The Two Leader: The Coach

The High Side of the Coach: Twos focus on the developmental needs of the team, helping others to develop their skills and abilities and advance in their careers.

The Low Side of the Coach: Twos can be intrusive, manipulative, show favoritism, and demand appreciation.

Where They Shine: *When they can help others thrive.* Twos love to play a supportive role and often see themselves as the power behind the throne that helps others be successful.

The Enneagram Emotional Competencies

As we have already discussed in Chapter Two, *emotional intelligence* is the ability to (1) identify your emotions and manage your responses to them, and (2) identify the emotions of others and manage your responses to them. The following *emotional competencies* are a set of sixteen specific capabilities based on emotional intelligence. They indicate how well Twos use emotional intelligence personally and socially.

PERSONAL COMPETENCIES

Self-Awareness

Self-Awareness: ability to identify one's thought processes, emotions, and skills
Typically: Twos spend more time focusing on their emotions than on their thought processes and skills. However, they tend to reject, at least outwardly, their own needs, and they find it difficult to identify and admit to certain emotions, especially negative ones. Twos tend to focus on other people; they tend to see themselves in relationship to others and identify their skills in relationship to how they can be used to help others.
When Stressed: Twos turn their focus outwardly on others even more, and their self-awareness decreases. They may overdo and dramatize their emotions and overreact to events and people. For example, a situation where they may be justifiably irritated may cause them to feel rage; they may have bouts of jealousy and self-pity that are not in proportion to the situation. They may become blind to how this behavior undermines their ability to help others.

Self-Confidence: confidence in one's powers and abilities
Typically: Twos are confident in their ability to take care of others, to get people to like them, to make sacrifices and to impose their will on others in a subtle, often pleasant way. They are willful in the sense that they assert their own value; they see themselves as good, loving people—and therefore deserving of the love and admiration of others. They are assertive and confident in their powers and abilities to get what they want.
When Stressed: Twos begin to lose confidence in their own abilities and may align themselves with more powerful, important people in an

attempt to reinforce their value and to feel more necessary to others. Oddly enough, stress makes Twos more assertive, making them appear more confident, and they become more demanding of support and attention, and begin to express their needs more openly.

Self-Management

Self-Control: restraint exercised over one's impulses, emotions or desires
Typically: Twos much prefer to be spontaneous and carefree rather than logical, practical and careful. They may see routines as restrictions to their freedom and spontaneity, which they guard dearly. They see themselves as emotional people and take pride in expressing their feelings. They may sometimes disregard boundaries—offering help, giving advice, or trying to make contact when it is not requested or appropriate.
When Stressed: Twos may struggle with respecting boundaries even more and can become frantic in their desire to be needed or to connect with or control people. They may find delaying gratification difficult and may buy things they cannot afford, eat foods that they should avoid, and so forth.

Adaptability: flexibility in handling change
Typically: Twos are open and receptive and they handle change best when they see themselves as being able to help others adapt to the change. When change is seen as an opportunity to help others, Twos handle it well. Their impulsiveness and desire for adventure also serves them well here. They can flex their style to meet the needs of the circumstance by being assertive, bold and cunning one moment and gentle and loving the next. Twos thrive when the change involves rescuing someone, impressing the boss, winning over someone or sacrificing for the company.
When Stressed: As Twos begin to feel less appreciated, they may resent others, feeling that no one sees or understands the sacrifices they have made to adapt to the needs and wants of others. They lose the ability to repress their anger at not being seen as important, helpful, and caring. They may increasingly seek to align themselves with people who can protect them and isolate them from any negative effects of change.

Trustworthiness: maintaining standards of honesty and integrity
Typically: Self-aware Twos are sincere, and they maintain high standards of honesty and integrity in their desire to be helpful and to have solid relationships. At their best they can establish clear boundaries and speak from an objective perspective with no expectation of reward for saying the right thing. However, as we have seen, they tend to flatter—a subtle form of dishonesty—to get people to like them. Their need to be needed often makes Twos say only what they think people want to hear.
When Stressed: Twos become more people pleasing, saying and behaving in whatever way they feel will garner the love and appreciation they desire. They may tend to become self-deceptive, not recognizing that their helping others is a way of manipulating them to gain approval. As stress increases, they may struggle with keeping confidences, using gossip as a way to get closer to others.

Optimism: ability to anticipate and expect the best possible outcome
Typically: Twos are generally optimistic. They believe that they are doing fine and that they have the ability to help others become fine as well. Tending to be pleasant, cheerful, and humorous, they like to see these qualities in others. If other people around them are not optimistic, Twos will make it their project to make them so.
When Stressed: Twos may take personally other peoples' lack of enthusiasm because they fear being seen as pessimists. They can take on a forced optimism and work to manufacture cheer. They sometimes create a façade of happiness and make a show of how happy and upbeat they are, believing that this is what people want to see.

Initiative: readiness to act on opportunities
Typically: Twos want to make an impact and to show their value. If an opportunity presents itself, they will generally be primed and ready for it. They want to be seen and approved of, and Twos cultivate an image of being ready, willing, and able in a variety of ways. They are assertive, but their self-image often requires them to downplay and mask their assertiveness. They like to be in control and tend to align themselves with people who have power and can get things done. Twos are ambitious, assertive in the face of a challenge, and generally ready to move when the right opportunity arises.
When Stressed: Twos develop a sense of entitlement and their initiative may take on a selfish tone. They may be less relaxed and trusting and may attempt to coerce people or try to force their will on

others. When highly stressed, their initiative takes on an obsessive quality and they may act out their repressed anger inappropriately.

Achievement Drive: striving to meet or improve a standard of excellence
Typically: Most Twos are competitive and concerned with excellence in whatever they undertake. It is important for them to do their job well. Some Twos are driven to be successful in a conventional way, but more often Twos do not have the kind of achievement drive that is normally associated with high-powered positions. They want to gain the respect and attention of others, including peers, bosses and, especially, of "that special someone." They are generally driven by professional or personal relationships more than by raw ambition.
When Stressed: Twos may begin to feel unappreciated and demand recognition from others. As stress mounts, they can become prideful and inflate their importance. If the recognition is not forthcoming, Twos may become rebellious and resistant to others' expectations.

Resiliency: capacity to endure in the face of obstacles
Typically: Twos see obstacles as an opportunity to help others and nurture those in need. They have a sincere desire to help distressed friends and co-workers and to be rescuers. While they are often steadfast friends to those facing obstacles, they may have difficulty facing their own obstacles. They may need to rely more and more on other people as obstacles increase, but Twos will usually hesitate to ask for help and often resent having to do so. They prefer that help be offered voluntarily.
When Stressed: Twos may hint at, complain about, or use some other indirect means to insist that others assist them in dealing with obstacles. They may expect special privileges and in the face of obstacles, stressed Twos often have an increased sense of entitlement and may even expect people to be at their beck and call. They often see tough times as an opportunity for people to repay them for the good deeds they have done.

SOCIAL COMPETENCIES

Attunement to Others

Empathy: awareness of and participation in others' feelings, ideas, and needs
Typically: Twos place high value on being aware of and participating in the lives of those they care about. They are able to sense the special

gifts of others and to anticipate what specific support and nurturing an individual may need. Intuitive about others' feelings, ideas, and needs, Twos seem to have an uncanny ability to read these in others. Self-aware Twos learn to put these gifts to great use and are often found in social work, the medical field, teaching, and human resources.

When Stressed: Twos focus on their own needs and may become demanding. They may become manipulative and pretend to be empathic when they are really trying to take care of themselves. Highly stressed Twos may become unaware of others' feelings, ideas, and needs, and may feel increasingly more entitled to be appreciated, applauded, and taken care of.

Political Awareness: reading a group's emotional currents and power relationships
Typically: Twos are excellent at reading both emotional currents and power relationships. They desire to have power—but usually through another—and are attuned to those who have it. They may hesitate to admit this desire, however. They make skilled second lieutenants, and often see themselves as "the power behind the thrown." They are astute at gauging the feelings of others and are often good at reading the emotional currents, passion, and direction a group is going.

When Stressed: Twos tend to lose their clarity around reading emotional currents and project their own needs, concerns, or shortcomings onto the group. For example, if they feel they are not being recognized, they will reframe this as the group not being recognized. This helps Twos avoid admitting their own needs.

Communication: listening openly and sending convincing messages
Typically: Twos are good listeners and are genuinely attentive to what others have to say. They tend to focus on others and are willing to share personal, often intimate, details about themselves. They are active listeners and tend to communicate with an enthusiasm that draws the listener in. They know how to make the person they are listening or speaking to feel that he or she is the only one in the room. Twos want to be supportive and help others grow and achieve their goals, and they communicate this convincingly. Twos generally have good interpersonal skills, seeing this as a way to connect with others.

When Stressed: Twos may become dramatic, overly emotional, and aggressive. They may lose interest in helping other people and become self-centered and uninterested in listening to others. They tend to dominate the conversation, leaving little space for others to respond. This is a way to keep the attention on them, as if to say, "It's finally *my* turn!"

Relationship Building

Cooperation: working with others toward shared goals
Typically: Twos seek to be a part of the lives of others and love to cooperate with teammates. While they sometimes enjoy working alone, they usually enjoy roles that require interaction with others. They want to share the best of themselves and help others to be their best; they do this by making people feel important, special, and valued. They make sure that everyone on the team is involved and acknowledged.

When Stressed: Twos may begin to feel unappreciated by other team members and may begin to complain about having to do so much for others. They tend to draw attention to the contributions they have made to others, the team, the company, and so forth. Under increased stress, Twos often feel that they have been overlooked and are entitled to special treatment.

Leadership: inspiring and leading individuals and groups
Typically: Twos display a curious contradiction around this competency. They want to impose their will on the environment, but Twos want to do so covertly and are often found in leadership roles behind the scenes. Twos generally do not want to be leaders in the conventional sense of the word because leaders risk alienating people, something that Twos are reluctant to do. Their leadership style tends to involve nurturing others, and they inspire by making people feel valuable.

When Stressed: Twos focus on the way they are perceived by others and thus have difficulty making hard decisions and keeping perspective. Because they worry about how the behavior of their followers or employees reflects on them, they can become controlling, critical and judgmental.

Influence: wielding effective tactics for persuasion
Typically: Twos intuitively know what others need to hear in order to feel secure, confident, and valued. Their bright, attentive nature makes them pleasant to be around, and makes it easy for them to be persuasive. People want to listen to what Twos have to say because it is generally upbeat, inspiring, and often exciting. They are masters at

influencing others through complimenting them, noticing their accomplishments, and praising their performance.

When Stressed: Twos begin to place more importance on their ability to exert their will but are less confident in their ability to do so. They may become manipulative, often cutting deals behind the scenes. They may treat people like pawns, using flattery, innuendo, rumors, and gossip to get people to do their bidding. They can become obsessed with aligning themselves with special, high-profile, and powerful people.

Conflict Management: Negotiating and resolving disputes
Typically: Twos strive to resolve impending disputes actively through being cooperative and helpful. They may at times be pushovers and allow people to take advantage of them in an effort to not make waves. Once drawn into conflict however, they may become assertive and are quite willing to stand up for themselves. They are good at resolving third-party disputes because they are good at seeing other perspectives and they want people to get along.
When Stressed: Twos may resist compromise and can be quite vocal in stating their case. They may project their own darker motives onto others and accuse people of being selfish, controlling and manipulative. Highly stressed Twos may become very aggressive, volatile, and combative.

The Awareness to Action Process

Improving Self-Awareness

Self-Awareness is an area where many Twos struggle. Unlocking the Two's full capacity for high performance often lies in improving in this competency. What follows is an example of how a Two might work on this key developmental area; it is not a literal "cook book" for all Twos, and you may find that improving performance in other competencies is more critical for you. The purpose of this example is to demonstrate how you might use the three steps of The Awareness to Action Process to identify *your* specific developmental areas and improve in those areas.

  Other competencies that Twos would do well to improve in are Self-Control and Self-Confidence. Self-Awareness, Self-Control, and Self-Confidence are interrelated and improvement in one often facilitates improvement in the other two. Self-Awareness is the ability to identify one's thought processes, emotions, and skills. It is also the ability to be able to be self-reflective and identify your needs rather than focusing on everyone else's needs. Self-Control involves restraint over one's impulses, emotions and desires, and the ability to think clearly and stay composed under pressure. Self-Confidence is confidence in one's powers and abilities, as well as the ability to espouse unpopular opinions. Self-awareness is essential for self-control, because we need to be aware of what thoughts, emotions, and skills need to be controlled. Self-confidence without self-awareness and self-control often leads to an expression of problems such as a hunger for power, an unrealistic need for recognition, or a relentless drive to be right, perfect, or successful.

When formulating your own action plan, work on one or two important goals at a time; create small steps that will move you toward each goal; go from easiest to most difficult, and celebrate your success.

Phase One: Build Awareness

Identify a goal.

- Improve performance in the emotional competency of Self-Awareness.

Identify your current patterns.

- "I usually focus on the needs of other people, and simply prefer not to look at negative emotions. I can distort or exaggerate my reactions to certain disappointing events and people. I also find it difficult to see what part I may have played in an argument or disagreement. People may see self-serving motives behind my actions, even when I feel I am trying to help people."

Phase Two: Develop Authenticity

Identify how your Preferred Strategy is in conflict with improving in this competency.

- "To me, Striving to be Connected usually means I am focused on others, and thus avoiding self-reflection. I prefer to align myself with other people and tend to identify myself with their thoughts, emotions, and skills. To improve in self-awareness means moving my focus from others to myself, which is in conflict with my Striving to be Connected.

Revise your strategy so that it incorporates improvement in this competency. (Remember that when Twos overdo their Striving to be Connected they might become dependent.)

- "I can connect to my own deepest needs and feelings by developing the ability to be aware of and express my own wants rather than trying to get others to fulfill them for me. Ultimately, this will enable me to truly connect with others without manipulation or dependence."

Phase Three: Take Action

Devise and Execute an Action Plan; be sure that it involves a goal, action steps, a person who will help monitor your success, and a timeline for completion. See Appendix C for a sample Action Plan. Sample action steps are listed below.

- Spend time alone and inquire into your own thoughts and feelings. There is no getting around it; the only way to develop self-awareness is to practice observing your inner landscape. Simply notice what emotions are present to your awareness, and how they determine what you see, think, and do.
- Practice observing your body, its aches and pains or lack thereof. That headache, backache, stomach problem, or bout of anxiety that you are trying to ignore may correspond to the way you ignore your own feelings or desires.
- Stop living for others. Ask yourself ten times a day, "What do *I* want and need?"
- Recognize that spending time with yourself is not selfish nor will it isolate you from others. Being aware of yourself will make you more aware and more connected to others.
- See Appendix B, General Recommendations for Growth.

CHAPTER SIX

TYPE THREE:
STRIVING TO BE OUTSTANDING

*The people who get on in this world are the people who get up and
look for the circumstances they want, and, if they can't
find them, make them.*
GEORGE BERNARD SHAW

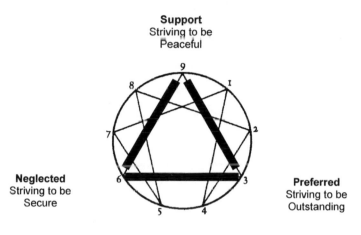

Support
Striving to be
Peaceful

Neglected
Striving to be
Secure

Preferred
Striving to be
Outstanding

Portrait of a Three

Mark is a salesman for a chemical distribution company. He has been
the top salesperson for five consecutive years. He attributes much of
his success to setting, as he puts it, "clear, measurable, and ambitious
goals," with the emphasis on *ambitious.* Working long hours,
traveling long distances, and volunteering for increasingly more
responsibility are what he expects of himself. "I'm never satisfied,"
he told us, "I'm used to breaking records at any company I work for,
but what I really aim for is setting the bar higher than anyone before
me has. I always want to be the best."

He is admired by management for his endless energy and
sales skills. "He's the kind of employee companies dream of," his
boss told us. "He works 'twenty four/ seven' and is always pushing to
achieve more."

Mark has the charm, appearance, and drive to be a success in
whatever he tries. He is the quintessential Type A personality and

knows it. "I'm one of the lucky people on the planet," he told us, "because I love to work. I get up in the morning and I'm energized. The more productive I can be the more I enjoy the day."

What Mark will not tell you is how well he sells himself. He sees himself much like a product, and like a product, he packages and presents himself in only the most flattering light. A consummate salesperson, he is able to create an image that customers and his boss want to see. "What good is being the best in your field if nobody knows it?" he'll ask. "I know what customers want, and I never hesitate to promise that I can deliver, no matter what it takes."

What it takes is often turmoil and frustration for the warehouse crew that must make good on his promises. "His customers might love Mark," said Dan, the plant manager, "but the crew has a real problem with him. No matter how many times he's told, no matter how many meetings we have about him, he still promises the moon. We have to ask people to work overtime at the last minute, and jump through hoops to bail him out. I wish he could just be honest with his customers about our delivery schedule. And I wish he could be honest with me," he adds. "He denies promising overnight deliveries, when I know he does it all the time and doesn't care how it affects morale. He'll tell you that the customer demanded the delivery date, or that they said they would go to our competitor. Sometimes, though, it just seems like he's trying to look good and to outdo the other sales guys."

Mark is highly task focused and often forgets to show empathy for his coworkers. He has difficulty relaxing because he always feels that there is too much work to be done. There is a restlessness in him that compels him to keep looking for some other project or task to tackle. While these qualities in many ways make Mark (like most workaholics) a desirable employee, they are sometimes detrimental to his relationships and Mark runs a high risk of eventual burnout.

Mark is a Three. Of course, not all Threes have exactly the same traits that Mark does, but some of his characteristics will resonate with you if you are a Three. You may also recognize some of these behaviors if you know a Three. Mark, like all Threes, is motivated to be outstanding.

The rest of this chapter explores the personality dynamics of Threes and shows how they can improve performance in the emotional competencies.

The Strategies

The Preferred Strategy: Striving to be Outstanding

Threes interact with the world by Striving to be Outstanding. Different Threes may use different words for "Striving to be Outstanding," such as wanting to be successful, accomplished, valuable, productive, etc. Regardless of the words they use, however, Threes work hard to exceed standards and be successful in whatever they undertake. They place a high value on productivity and presenting an image of being a winner. Threes believe that they must always accomplish their goals and achieve more than the average person.

When Threes overdo their Preferred Strategy, "outstanding" becomes distorted into "attention-seeking." Stressed Threes deal with the world by making sure that others are aware of their accomplishments, possessions, and personal attributes, such as their looks, intelligence, or expertise. Stressed Threes may place more value on image than substance.

The Neglected Strategy: Striving to be Secure

The strategy at Point Six, Striving to be Secure, in some ways contradicts the Three's desire to be outstanding. Being "secure" by finding acceptance within the group, including the security of the average job, the average house, etc., as Sixes often do, makes it difficult to stand out. Therefore, Threes become uncomfortable with this strategy and "neglect" it. Rather than seeing the full value of security through fitting in, Threes distort it and see it as *mediocrity*. They believe that if they become too secure—comfortable with the status quo—they will become lazy and mediocre and lose their drive to be outstanding.

This is not to say that Threes are not security conscious in other ways. In fact, their Striving to be Outstanding is often in the service of security. High achievement ensures that they will be valued at work; success ensures that they are financially secure; having social grace ensures that people will like them. Threes often struggle, however, with trying to balance security *by fitting in,* (which entails slowing down), with security *by standing out*, (which entails speeding up).

The Contradiction: Achievement vs. Anxiety

The neglect of the natural and healthy desire to be secure causes Threes to act out the Neglected Strategy in subtle and predictable ways. Threes are usually achievement-oriented but sometimes give in to their repressed desire for security and experience anxiety. For example, they may actively seek recognition and praise from others as assurance that they are doing a good job. When Threes become aware that they are acting this way, they will quickly revert to their typical Three behavior of acting self-assured and in-control.

The Support Strategy: Striving to be Peaceful

Threes use Striving to be Peaceful, the strategy found at Point Nine, to reinforce being outstanding. They cultivate an air of graceful effort and the confident, polished demeanor of a professional in action. They rarely become flustered; no task seems too difficult and no goal seems unreachable. However, under stress Threes may also become withdrawn and passively look to others for cues on how they should think, feel, or act. The peacefulness hides their anxiety about being able to meet all of the challenges they have taken on.

Threes At Their Best

When Threes are at their best, they use all three strategies naturally and appropriately rather than in the habitual patterns described above. They are accomplished without feeling the need to bring attention to their accomplishments; they are secure and comfortable without fear of being mediocre; and they are calm and peaceful while being open about their insecurities.

Threes At a Glance

Examples of Threes: Oprah Winfrey, Arnold Schwarzenegger, Tom Cruise, Christopher Reeve, Brooke Shields, Dick Clark, Michael Jordan.

Chief Asset: *Achievement.* Threes have a unique capacity for self-actualization and success in whatever endeavors they pursue.

What They Like in Others: Prestige, success, efficiency.

What They Dislike in Others: Failure, emotions, indifference to their achievements.

How They Frustrate Others: Self-centeredness, overselling themselves, cutting corners.

Approach to Problem Solving: "Let's just concentrate on getting this done."

Belief About Work: "Things work best when I'm given a chance to shine."

How Others See Threes: Ambitious, successful, goal-oriented, focused, competitive, but sometimes egotistical, political, shallow, deceptive, and attention-seeking.

Threes Get Into Trouble When They Tell Themselves: "My value is based on my actions and accomplishments and the way I am perceived by others."

Blind Spot: *Inauthenticity.* Threes are often unaware of their tendency to be inauthentic and its affect on their relationships. Because of their desire to put a positive spin on everything they do, Threes fall into the habit of deceiving themselves, and sometimes others. Because they are pragmatists, they look for the best solution and the most effective action even if it involves shading the truth. They do not consider their deceit as lying, but rather as reframing or "spinning."

The Three Leader: The Pacesetter

The High Side of the Pacesetter: Threes inspire others by setting an example of high performance and excellence.

The Low Side of the Pacesetter: Threes can place unrealistically high expectations on people and may not consider the needs and values of others.

Where They Shine: *In the spotlight.* Threes love to be noticed for their accomplishments and generally take opportunities to have their achievements noticed by others.

The Enneagram Emotional Competencies

As we have already discussed in Chapter Two, *emotional intelligence* is the ability to (1) identify your emotions and manage your responses to them, and (2) identify the emotions of others and manage your responses to them. The following *emotional competencies* are a set of sixteen specific capabilities based on emotional intelligence. They indicate how well Threes use emotional intelligence personally and socially.

PERSONAL COMPETENCIES

Self-Awareness

Self-Awareness: ability to identify one's thought processes, emotions, and skills
Typically: Threes are much more aware of their skills and thought processes than their emotions. They are particularly good at knowing what their strengths are and capitalizing on them. They tend to avoid complicated emotions, however, often seeming unsure of what they are feeling, and looking for clues from others as to what they should be feeling.
When Stressed: Threes focus on creating and supporting an idealized image of themselves and may overestimate their skills, often taking on too many projects in an attempt to appear highly accomplished. They lose touch with their emotions even more, and their anxiety may cause them to be unsure of what their opinions are.

Self-Confidence: confidence in one's powers and abilities
Typically: Threes work hard to be good at whatever they do, so they build a track record of success that breeds self-confidence. Confident in their ability to take care of themselves and to get things done, Threes thrive in situations where goals must be met and challenges abound. Threes are also independent and learned early how to look out for their own self-interests. Their self-confident, "I-can-do-it" attitude is inspirational to people, and is one of the traits that people most admire about them.
When Stressed: Stress may trigger insecurity in Threes and they may begin to doubt their abilities and value. They usually respond to this self-doubt by pushing themselves to accomplish more and more, believing that the only way they will fit in and be accepted is if they

are winners, top producers, or "stars." Threes may take on more than they can possibly accomplish, believing that this will increase their value or that success in something will put them back on solid footing. Often, however, this overreaching leads to mistakes and undermines their confidence.

Self-Management

Self-Control: restraint exercised over one's impulses, emotions or desires
Typically: Threes focus on what people think of them, and they make calculated efforts to maintain both their self-image and the image they present to the world. They often appear serious and measured and excel at delaying gratification in order to reach a goal. They can mold themselves to a specific image, which may involve such things as dieting, bodybuilding, getting the right degree, and meeting the right people. Threes will not often be found lounging in front of the TV with a box of chocolates. They exercise whatever discipline they feel is appropriate to meet their goals.
When Stressed: Threes can become desperate in their desire to be seen in a positive light; doing so may distort their behavior and they may give in to impulses that they normally would not, such as being deceptive and cutting corners. Highly stressed Threes may become overly competitive and may step on toes or act unethically to get what they want.

Adaptability: flexibility in handling change
Typically: Threes are probably the most adaptable of the nine types. Because they are pragmatic and focused on end-results, Threes will skillfully adapt to the requirements of their environment in order to get the task done. Threes often see their ability to change on a moment's notice as a way of meeting challenges, and they highly value this competency. A change or a detour can be viewed as a way to rise to the occasion and show that they are a cut above the rest.
When Stressed: Threes become even more focused on the wants and expectations of the environment and become chameleon-like—sometimes becoming too adaptable and not appearing to have their own stance. They may become overly political and may do or say whatever they feel will win people over or help them be seen in a good light.

Trustworthiness: maintaining standards of honesty and integrity
Typically: Self-aware Threes tend to be ethical, hard working and industrious. However, many Threes have a blind spot in this competency because they have a tendency to "spin" interpretations of events to make things come out in the best light. Their marketing mentality may cause them to paint rosy pictures of situations or events. For example, they may emphasize the good news over the bad news, play up what people have in common, and downplay obstacles or differences. Threes may exaggerate their own accomplishments and focus on putting their best foot forward. They are always on their best behavior around people who count, like their boss or upper management.
When Stressed: In their concern about their image, stressed Threes may stretch the truth, take credit for ideas and accomplishments of others, or misrepresent themselves. They may try so hard to paint a good picture that others may feel they are being lied to even when the Three is telling the truth.

Optimism: ability to anticipate and expect the best possible outcome
Typically: Their high self-confidence and history of accomplishment predisposes Threes to being optimistic about the future. They believe they can accomplish what they set their minds to and that they can inspire others to do the same. Threes do not tolerate failure in themselves, so there is little room for anything but positive anticipations and outcomes. It should be noted that Threes have the kind of optimism that relies on their own skills and abilities to accomplish goals rather than on an innate confidence in ideas such as the goodness of life or fate. They tend to believe that things will work out fine if they are involved, but they may be doubtful of others.
When Stressed: Threes stay optimistic, but they buckle down and work harder. They may become more obsessive about depending only on themselves, feeling that others have their own agendas and self-interest in mind and that these agendas may get in the way of their goals. They remain optimistic about their abilities but become even less trusting in the ability and commitment of others.

Initiative: readiness to act on opportunities
Typically: Threes feel as if they are "hard wired" to work toward success and achievement. They are constantly looking for opportunities to take the initiative and to demonstrate their value. Visibility, excellence of execution, and recognition are motivators for them, and they are masters at being in the right place at the right time.

Their skills at networking, communication, and reading people serve them well in this competency because they often seem to have an infrastructure in place to help them get started on a project. They know whom to call to get a project going and what channels to go through to get it done quickly.

When Stressed: Threes may take too much initiative and aggressively take on too many projects. They lose the ability to say no and may experience quality problems in their efforts to look as if they are outworking and outperforming everyone else. Under increased stress they may look for bigger, higher profile challenges to take on in an effort to increase their visibility. Highly stressed Threes may even create problems to solve in an attempt to be seen as invaluable by important people.

Achievement Drive: striving to meet or improve a standard of excellence

Typically: Threes are natural goal setters who thrive on the challenge of improving a standard of excellence. They want to be the best and to be acknowledged as such. They love to compete with others and are great at trying to break existing records. This brings them the sort of approval and validation that Threes desire so much. Threes are also very aware of existing standards and they are willing to recreate themselves, if necessary, to exceed them.

When Stressed: Threes may become frantic in a desire to achieve more and more. In an effort to appear that they are exceeding goals, they may exaggerate their achievements. They may lash out at others who they feel may jeopardize their ability to be successful.

Resiliency: capacity to endure in the face of obstacles

Typically: Threes usually see obstacles as challenges and meeting them fuels their competitiveness. Threes will do whatever it takes to overcome obstacles and avoid failure or the appearance of failure. They have a strong belief in themselves and their ability to bring things to closure, so they generally have a high capacity to overcome obstacles. They take pride in showcasing what they have accomplished against the odds.

When Stressed: If a project has low visibility, or if stressed Threes believe it will not advance their career, they may take the easy way out and try to delegate the dirty work of dealing with the obstacle to others, disavow themselves of the project, and, in short, bail out. Stressed Threes usually have little interest in taking on projects that do not have a high potential for success, recognition, or advancement, and they avoid work that may show them in less than their best light.

SOCIAL COMPETENCIES

Attunement to Others

Empathy: awareness of and participation in others' feelings, ideas, and needs
Typically: Threes are often scanning others for cues on how to act and may therefore be aware of others' feelings, needs and ideas. Their lack of contact with—or trust of—their own feelings may make it difficult, however, for Threes to actually participate in these feelings. They may also regard feelings as a distraction from being efficient and getting the maximum amount of work done, and Threes may become frustrated with those who let emotions get in the way of achieving a goal.
When Stressed: Threes shut down their emotions even more, and their ability to empathize diminishes. They become uncomfortable around emotional people and try to get as much distance from them as possible. Their competitive streak comes out and they may put their own needs ahead of others'.

Political Awareness: reading a group's emotional currents and power relationships
Typically: Threes are not as good at reading emotional currents as they are at reading power relationships. They struggle with reading emotional currents because they are often not in touch with their own emotions. They tend to downplay the value of emotions and disregard the impact of emotions on themselves and the group. They are, however, very good at reading power relationships. They are very aware of who holds power, who can positively or negatively impact their career, and who can provide them with the resources they need to get a job done.
When Stressed: Their ambition may cloud their judgment, and Threes may become too Machiavellian—prone to political manipulations and backroom deals. They may become unconcerned with emotional currents and often step on toes and make enemies along the way to pursuing their goal, which can, ironically, end up being the downfall of their "political" ambitions.

Communication: listening openly and sending convincing messages
Typically: Threes are usually good listeners, but sometimes they use this skill only within a limited range of topics. They may listen in order to find common ground they can use to create beneficial

relationships. They listen for and remember names, titles, and relationships. They are charming, charismatic, inspiring, and appear earnest. They know how to make people feel valuable and optimistic and are generally good at inspiring others. However, they are generally better sending than listening to messages.

When Stressed: Threes may become overly focused on their own accomplishments and lose interest in communicating well with others, especially subordinates and peers. Instead, they focus their attention strictly on people they consider important, such as bosses. Other people sometimes feel that Threes are selling to them even when they do not need to, which creates distrust in listeners. In the excitement of the moment, stressed Threes may also make promises that they later forget and fail to keep.

Relationship Building

Cooperation: working with others toward shared goals
Typically: Threes excel as individual contributors but may struggle with cooperation. Threes are such hard workers that they may become exasperated with those who cannot keep pace or perform at the high level the Three expects. They cooperate in their own way by being great organizers and goal setters, but they are most effective at inspiring others by setting an example rather than by working in tandem. Threes may fall into the pattern of appearing to cooperate and take on tasks on team projects, only to later find themselves over-committed and unable to follow through. Conversely, they may take on the majority of the work on a team and eventually become resentful and reluctant to continue to be part of the group.

When Stressed: Threes can become frustrated with having to share goals and may begin to view teammates as incompetent and as not worthy of being on a team with them. They often fear that others will hold them back or reflect poorly on them. Stressed Threes want to see themselves as better than others and may even compete with people on their own team.

Leadership: inspiring and leading individuals and groups
Typically: Threes are good at setting goals and leading by example. They can boost confidence in others and inspire people to accomplish common objectives. People are often inspired by their achievements. People may want to follow them because they are appealing, likeable, charming, and charismatic. However, their stance may change

depending upon political expediency, and others may not feel the sense of certainty they often seek in a leader.

When Stressed: Threes' struggles with inauthenticity can weaken their ability to lead. People see their increasing self-interest and begin to distrust stressed Threes, often feeling that they are being used for the Three's own agenda. Highly stressed Threes may abandon people who become political liabilities, an action that instills resentment and cynicism in their remaining followers.

Influence: wielding effective tactics for persuasion

Typically: Threes can be very persuasive and are often successful in sales and marketing roles. More than any other type, they know how to project an image that is desirable to others—whether it is for themselves, their ideas, or their products. They are also good at "reading" their listener and changing tactics in midstream if necessary. They usually know the right thing to say to the right people at the right time in order to get their ideas across.

When Stressed: They are still fairly effective at persuasion but may become deceptive and may get caught in their deception. As stress increases, their need for approval and admiration increases and lends urgency to persuading others that they are more successful, important, or capable than they appear to be.

Conflict Management: Negotiating and resolving disputes

Typically: Threes have the capacity to resolve conflict unemotionally, and they can stick to the facts and not take things too personally. However, most Threes see conflict as an impediment to getting things done and work to avoid it whenever possible. Conflict also involves highly charged emotions—which make Threes uncomfortable. Threes may see the efforts involved in resolving disputes as a waste of time and simply avoid the source of conflict in the interest of efficiency.

When Stressed: Threes focus more on winning than on compromise, and they may begin to think win/lose rather than win/win. They can become combative, arrogant, and evasive. To avoid a direct, often messy confrontation, they may resort to going behind people's backs to garner support from influential people.

The Awareness to Action Process

Improving Cooperation

Cooperation is an area where many Threes struggle. Unlocking the Three's full capacity for high performance often lies in improving in this competency. What follows is an example of how a Three might work on this key developmental area; it is not a literal "cook book" for all Threes, and you may find that improving performance in other competencies is more critical for you. The purpose of this example is to demonstrate how you might use the three steps of The Awareness to Action Process to identify *your* specific developmental areas and improve in those areas.

Other competencies that Threes would do well to improve in are Trustworthiness and Empathy. Cooperation, Trustworthiness, and Empathy are interrelated and improvement in one often facilitates improvement in the other two. Cooperation involves the ability to work with others toward shared goals. Trustworthiness is the foundation of building relationships, and means that you are accountable and dependable to deliver on your commitments. Empathy is the awareness of and participation in others' feelings, ideas, and needs. Both Trustworthiness and Empathy are key ingredients in Cooperation.

When formulating your own action plan, work on one or two important goals at a time; create small steps that will move you toward each goal; go from easiest to most difficult, and celebrate your success.

Phase One: Build Awareness
Identify a goal.

- Improve performance in the emotional competency of Cooperation.

Identify your current behaviors.

- "I'm more naturally an individual contributor, rather than a team member. Sharing goals with others is difficult for me, as is sharing the acknowledgement that comes from succeeding. I generally feel that I perform at a higher level than others and find it hard to cooperate with people who I feel aren't pulling their weight."

Phase Two: Develop Authenticity

Identify how your Preferred Strategy is in conflict with improving in this competency.

- "To me, Striving to be Outstanding means being the most productive person on my team, and being acknowledged as such. I want to stand out from others, and not be seen as part of the group, especially if it is only average. Also, my tendency to reframe things so that I'm seen as the best on my team is in conflict with cooperation."

Revise your strategy so that it incorporates improvement in this competency. (Remember that when Threes overdo their Striving to be Outstanding they can become attention seeking and may put more value on image than substance.)

- "Being Outstanding means accomplishing not only my personal goals but the goals of the organization, and I can do this most effectively by working toward shared goals with others. Building relationships that are essential to success depends on cooperation."

Phase Three: Take Action

Devise and Execute an Action Plan; be sure that it involves a goal, action steps, a person who will help monitor your success, and a timeline for completion. See Appendix C for a sample Action Plan. Sample action steps are listed below.

- Compete with the competition, not your coworkers. Your success will ultimately depend upon how well you can get along with people on your team. Don't undermine or criticize their accomplishments as a way to bolster your own image. Learn to work with others and to share the limelight. Don't take credit for things you have not done personally.
- Share the glory and share the power. Resisit the temptation to dictate the end result of a project or meeting. It is OK to let others on your team take the lead and to articulate *their* goals. Cooperation means really listening to the ideas of others and creating shared goals and values.
- Cooperation involves being trustworthy. Be absolutely honest with progress reports and sales numbers. Don't make promises to team members that you can't keep.

- Be a team member: share your expertise, resources, information, and exuberance with others.
- Recognize that not everyone is motivated to work "24/7" like you. That doesn't mean they are slackers or not committed.
- See Appendix B, General Recommendations for Growth.

CHAPTER SEVEN

TYPE FOUR: *STRIVING TO BE UNIQUE*

*It seems to me we can never give up longing and wishing while we
are alive. There are certain things we feel to be beautiful and good,
and we must hunger for them.*
GEORGE ELIOT

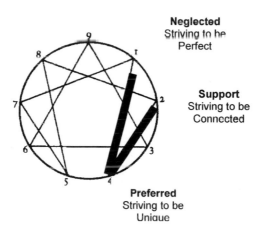

Neglected
Striving to be
Perfect

Support
Striving to be
Connected

Preferred
Striving to be
Unique

Portrait of a Four

Clara's office stands out from everyone else's in her department. As
you walk through her door you are greeted by an interesting piece of
art: an original painting of a woman, her hair long and wild, her
clothing elegant yet rebellious, and her face a bit mysterious. One
looks at the woman in the painting and thinks, "This is different."

Clara is the marketing communications manager for a large
manufacturing company. She is responsible for the creation of
marketing brochures, letters to clients, product literature, and any
communication from her company to the public. For the last three
years she has been in charge of designing and maintaining the
company's web site. Clara describes this project as "demanding,
exciting, and rewarding." The website, like all of the products she

develops, taps into her creativity and brings out her passion for excellence.

"I like working for Clara," a graphic designer in her department told us. "She knows what she wants, and has a clear vision of how things should be presented. She's passionate about her work, people, relationships, and life in general."

However, Clara will tell you that she often feels "like a fish out of water" at work. "I'm very conscious of the creative quality of what I do," she said, "and my tastes tend to lean toward the artistic, and the quirky, and are often not very 'corporate.' But I'm a marketing person and the goal is not beauty but sales. This job has been very good for me; it's forced me to be 'bottom-line' oriented."

Her boss has few complaints. "My frustration with Clara is that she's so much better than she thinks she is," he told us. "She's one of the few people I know who evaluates herself lower than others do. Most people inflate their accomplishments and talent but Clara doesn't recognize her potential. She can linger on the past and on the negative too much. She's a great manager, and understands people really well."

But there is another side to Clara. "She's not always the sensitive, gentle person she appears to be," said a coworker. "She can be very temperamental and self-absorbed. She can be so much into doing her own thing that she doesn't check in with other people in the office, and doesn't seem to hear their feedback."

Clara tends to look for what's missing, not only in her work, but also in herself, and in her personal life. She works hard at accomplishing her goals as long as they have an emotional significance for her. She thrives in an environment where she can maintain her individuality and be appreciated for her contributions. There is a yearning in her that pushes her to strive for higher levels of productivity and quality. That yearning can also be seen in her longing for just the right relationship, the person who sees and appreciates her special qualities and uniqueness.

Clara is a Four. Of course, not all Fours have exactly the same traits that Clara does, but some of her characteristics will resonate with you if you are a Four. You may also recognize some of these behaviors if you know a Four. Clara, like all Fours, is motivated by striving to be unique.

The rest of this chapter explores the personality dynamics of Fours and shows how they can improve performance in the emotional competencies.

The Strategies

The Preferred Strategy: Striving to be Unique

Fours interact with the world by Striving to be Unique. Different Fours may use different words for "Striving to be Unique," such as wanting to be different, creative, or understood; striving to find or express themselves; etc. Regardless of the words they use, however, Fours are creative, reflective, and strive to approach their lives in fresh and interesting ways. They gravitate toward things and experiences that are elegant, refined, or unusual.

When Fours overdo their Preferred Strategy, "uniqueness" becomes distorted into "isolation." Stressed Fours deal with the world by withdrawing from those who don't "understand" them—which feels like almost everyone to the stressed Four. They can become remote, melancholic, and non-communicative.

The Neglected Strategy: Striving to be Perfect

The strategy at Point One, Striving to be Perfect, in some ways contradicts the Four's desire to be unique. Perfection, to the Four, implies a certain homogeneity and sameness, which the Four wishes to avoid. Therefore, Fours become uncomfortable with this strategy and "neglect" it. Rather than seeing the full value of Striving to be Perfect, Fours distort it and see it as *repression*. They may fear that if they do not put their own special touch on their world and their experiences they are in some way being inauthentic and that their creativity will be stifled.

This is not to say that Fours are incapable of being logical, insightful, and intellectually precise. In fact, Fours can be excellent advisors who make clear and objective observations. However, they are often more comfortable advising others than they are making clear and definitive decisions about matters in which they are directly involved.

The Contradiction: Nonconformity vs. Rigidity

The neglect of the natural and healthy desire to fit in, to be accepted, and "perfect" just as they are, causes Fours to act out the Neglected Strategy in subtle and predictable ways. Fours are usually nonconformists, but sometimes they can be very rigid. For example, they can be perfectionistic and intolerant of others who do not act "the right way." When Fours become aware that they are acting this way they will quickly revert to their typical "Four-ish" behavior of being emotionally sensitive and seeing themselves as flawed or out of the mainstream.

The Support Strategy: Striving to be Connected

Fours use Striving to be Connected, the strategy found at Point Two, to reinforce being unique. They use their ability to understand human nature to build relationships with interesting, talented, and desirable people. Fours are often charming people with a wide range of interests and tastes that they like to discuss with like-minded people. However, under stress they may depend on their attachments to others to make them feel complete, and lack the confidence to make decisions without the approval of people they deem important. They can also become possessive and emotionally dependent on others, holding unrealistic expectations for relationships.

Fours At Their Best

When Fours are at their best they use all three of the strategies naturally and appropriately rather than in the habitual patterns described above. They are creative and independent without artificial "uniqueness;" they are rational and logical without being demanding and critical of others; and they are open and connected to others without becoming dependent on them.

Fours At a Glance

Examples of Fours: Steve Jobs, Johnny Depp, Joni Mitchell, Edgar Allen Poe, Neil Young, Prince Charles, Judy Garland, Howard Stern.

Chief Asset: *Originality.* Fours have a heightened ability to see the uniqueness and specialness in themselves and others. They are great creators and appreciators of beauty and originality.

What They Like in Others: Refinement, sensitivity, creativity.

What They Dislike in Others: Coarseness, conformity, superficiality.

How They Frustrate Others: Moodiness, withdrawing, self-absorption.

Approach to Problem Solving: "I'm going to do this in a way that no one has ever done it before."

Belief About Work: "Things work best when I have the opportunity to put my own touch on them."

How Others See Fours: Empathic, creative, unique, and refined, but sometimes moody, dramatic, self-absorbed, and melancholic.

Fours Get Into Trouble When They Tell Themselves: "I'll never get what I truly want, but I must not stop hoping that someone or something will rescue me."

Blind Spot: *Self absorption.* Fours are often unaware of their tendency to be self absorbed and its affect on their relationships. They find their own lives and internal states far more interesting than anybody else's. Because they feel they have been cheated by life, but no one else has, they feel that the focus should be on them and their problems.

The Four Leader: The Visionary

The High Side of the Visionary: Fours create a vision of what the organization can be and move others toward a shared dream.

The Low Side of the Visionary: Fours can be impractical or become dispirited and resentful when their dream is not shared.

Where They Shine: *In creative environments.* Fours love opportunities to express their originality and creativity, so they do well in situations where they can add their own flare to projects.

The Enneagram Emotional Competencies

As we have already discussed in Chapter Two, *emotional intelligence* is the ability to (1) identify your emotions and manage your responses to them, and (2) identify the emotions of others and manage your responses to them. The following *emotional competencies* are a set of sixteen specific capabilities based on emotional intelligence. They indicate how well Fours use emotional intelligence personally and socially.

PERSONAL COMPETENCIES

Self-Awareness

Self-Awareness: ability to identify one's thought processes, emotions, and skills
Typically: Fours are probably the most self-aware type, especially when it comes to their thought processes and emotions. Highly developed Fours have a natural clarity and precision in discerning different variations in their emotions, such as the difference between sadness and depression. Their focus of attention is on their mental and emotional state, so they are naturally very aware of them. They do, however, sometimes have doubt in their abilities. They are concerned that others do not appreciate their unique skills and contributions, and they may begin to question these themselves.
When Stressed: Fours may become lost in their emotions or overwhelmed by highly emotional events. They lose clarity and may begin to either over-dramatize their emotions or become paralyzed in the attempt to discover exactly what they are feeling. Under stress, they may have a tendency to alternately inflate their abilities or lose confidence in their skills.

Self-Confidence: confidence in one's powers and abilities
Typically: Fours generally have a high degree of confidence in their ability to recognize and understand their own needs and the needs of others. They also have confidence in their creative abilities—their gift for adding uniqueness and flair to whatever they undertake. However, even high-functioning Fours sometimes feel that they do not quite fit into certain work environments and that they are lacking some competencies that others seem to have. This sense that they do not fit in undermines their general sense of confidence.

When Stressed: Fours fall into a pattern of comparing themselves to others and seeking out ways they fail to measure up. They may be prone to bouts of self-pity, feeling that no one understands or appreciates them for the valuable qualities they do have. Their negative self-image may get in the way of their promoting themselves or taking risks. Sometimes, stressed Fours may begin to overcompensate for their belief that they are flawed and begin to act in an arrogant and grandiose way.

Self-Management

Self-Control: restraint exercised over one's impulses, emotions or desires
Typically: Fours work hard to control what they reveal of themselves to others. They have a fear that if they reveal their real self, they will be found wanting—seen as lacking in skills and talents compared to other people. Therefore, their behavior is usually measured and proper, and they often take on an air of refinement. It should be noted that some Fours flaunt a seeming lack of inhibition. They rebel against the norms and standards of society and feel that they can only truly express themselves if they give in to their impulses and whims. This rebellion, however, often seems calculated and measured.
When Stressed: Fours restraint starts to falter and they have more difficulty controlling their emotions. Highly stressed Fours may fall victim to dramatic outbursts of anger, self-pity, or jealousy. Weary of trying to be proper, stressed Fours start to give into their impulses, may begin to disregard rules and procedures, and may become openly—and genuinely—rebellious.

Adaptability: flexibility in handling change
Typically: Like most of the other types, Fours respond to change depending on how they view it. They will welcome a change that they feel allows them more freedom to express themselves. Fours are autonomous and do not like to be limited by their environment or told what to do by others. They may resist change when they believe it places restrictions on them and limits their ability to express themselves.
When Stressed: Fours tend to rebel against almost any change, especially change that seems to them to be petty, insignificant, and arbitrary. Stressed Fours tend to take change personally, as if it were specifically designed to make their lives more difficult and restricted.

They tend not to crusade against change actively, but to rebel by becoming moody, brooding, and passive-aggressive.

Trustworthiness: *maintaining standards of honesty and integrity*
Typically: Most Fours set high standards of honesty and integrity. Life is a work of art to Fours, and they try to live with refinement. Part of this refinement tends to be living by a set of rules that they try to adhere to. Self-aware Fours would not dream of betraying the trust of others. Fours are busy marching to their own drummer, so they feel that they do not need to lie. Because their inner life may be turbulent, Fours have a tendency to look for certain things that are reliable and they can feel some sense of control over. Honesty and integrity is one of these areas—keeping their word makes them feel grounded and secure.
When Stressed: Fours have a tendency to have a Jekyll-and-Hyde quality around trustworthiness. Their poor impulse control under stress may allow them to disobey the rules. Stressed Fours feel unappreciated and unacknowledged and may feel that they have the right to change the rules at their own discretion. At the same time, stressed Fours tend to place high expectations for integrity on others and react angrily when they are not met.

Optimism: *ability to anticipate and expect the best possible outcome*
Typically: The enjoyment that Fours find in exploring their darker emotions makes them appear to others to be more pessimistic than they may actually be. They find meaning and richness in melancholy and a serious exploration of their emotional states. When they are at their best, however, they can transform this exploration into great beauty and deep understanding.
When Stressed: Fours may develop a conviction that the world is a cold and unsympathetic place. Their sense that they are flawed and missing out on the happiness that others possess sets them up to be disappointed and pessimistic. They can become increasingly pessimistic about their capacity to get things done, and they may feel unappreciated by others.

Initiative: *readiness to act on opportunities*
Typically: Fours tend to do well in entrepreneurial environments; they are not fond of following rules or being forced to fit into other people's plans. If they can find an endeavor that allows them to express themselves, they tend to do well in taking initiative. However, in a normal work setting, the self-doubt of typical Fours can hinder or undermine their ability to take advantage of opportunities. They often

feel the need to fully process their emotions and options before acting, and thus Fours run the risk of missing out on opportunities.

When Stressed: The more time Fours spend processing their emotions, the less initiative they will show. They can become mired in their personal creative effort but have trouble bringing their ideas into fruition in a pragmatic way. They also tend to lose interest in engaging with the world, thus even further diminishing their initiative.

Achievement Drive: striving to meet or improve a standard of excellence

Typically: Fours are concerned with excellence if the standard is one that involves personal expression. However, they are often unconcerned with mundane—and, to them, meaningless—standards, policies, and rules. The creative nature of Fours drives them to try new approaches, to stretch their creative muscles, and to be excellent at what they do. This orientation also makes them better suited for strategic thinking than for tactical action.

When Stressed: Fours may shut down and become introspective rather than engaging with or making an effort to improve things. They may lose interest in pursuing high standards and become pessimistic about their ability to meet, let alone exceed, standards. Highly stressed Fours may adopt a fatalistic attitude and convince themselves that they are simply not up to meeting the standards of the workplace.

Resiliency: capacity to endure in the face of obstacles

Typically: At times, Fours may see the business world as an obstacle to expressing themselves, which is why there sometimes seem to be fewer Fours in the corporate setting than other types. Sometimes, Fours may seem to find comfort in obstacles, as if they support their worldview that life is unfair to them and full of sadness. They may complain and over-dramatize their situation and may be hesitant to take action to overcome the obstacles.

When Stressed: Fours use obstacles as an opportunity to withdraw from others. Often, stressed Fours need time to be alone and to recharge. They also use obstacles as a way to verify their belief that they are defective and must work harder to function in a normal work setting than most people. As obstacles mount, they may try to align themselves with a rescuer who will help them overcome their obstacles.

SOCIAL COMPETENCIES

Attunement to Others

Empathy: awareness of and participation in others' feelings, ideas, and needs
Typically: Fours are very empathic. They are interested in their own feelings, ideas, and needs and can easily relate to those of others. Fours do not shy away from emotions and problems like some of the other types will—in fact, they generally enjoy discussing them. Because they understand themselves and feel their own pain, anxiety, and sorrow so acutely, they can readily relate and sympathize with others. Self-aware Fours are deeply caring and generally want to help other people.
When Stressed: Fours struggle with feeling empathy for others because their absorption with their own problems leaves little room for the problems of others. They also tend to become rigid in their views and demanding—two qualities that impede empathy. They may minimize what other people are going through, feeling that their own pain, sadness, and disappointment is more profound than that of others.

Political Awareness: reading a group's emotional currents and power relationships
Typically: Because Fours are so in touch with and interested in their own emotional currents, they are generally good at reading the group's currents. They excel at understanding the group's emotional status, morale, and who is in favor or out of favor with the boss. They notice power relationships, especially those that affect them directly. They are acutely aware of inequities in the system, such as who is being mistreated and who is gaining special favor.
When Stressed: Fours start to lose touch with the group's emotional currents because their focus turns to their own emotions. They can become self-absorbed and simply ignore others. They may see the political arena as crass, unsophisticated, and unrefined. Stressed Fours at best are indifferent to office politics; at worst they are contemptible of it.

Communication: listening openly and sending convincing messages
Typically: When they are engaged, Fours tend to be good communicators. They are good listeners who are emotionally available to others and enjoy discussing others' problems. They often

do not enjoy small talk, and if they are bored with a topic they will not hesitate to disengage. They do enjoy talking about weightier subjects, such as art, philosophy, religion, etc., and often get quite passionate about their views and opinions. This passion is often very convincing and inspiring to others.

When Stressed: Fours may become self-absorbed, and their communication tends to be all about them. They may take pleasure in giving negative feedback and pointing out other people's flaws, especially when they feel that they have been hurt somehow. On the other hand, they do not take criticism well. Stressed Fours are easily offended, taking even constructive criticism personally and becoming angry with the person who delivers it.

Relationship Building

Cooperation: working with others toward shared goals
Typically: Fours generally prefer being soloists to being team members. They take pride in being self-sufficient and not depending on others. Their self-image is based on being unique, original, and independent, and they generally get less satisfaction out of creating something with others than they do in creating something by themselves. Their tendency to feel misunderstood makes them hesitate to openly express or expose themselves, a tendency that hinders cooperation.

When Stressed: Fours go to great lengths to avoid cooperation and interaction with others. For stressed Fours, security lies in withdrawing from the group and into their own thoughts and feelings. It is very difficult for stressed Fours to work toward shared goals because doing so is antithetical to their expression of individuality.

Leadership: inspiring and leading individuals and groups
Typically: Fours' ability to think strategically would seem to predispose them to be good leaders, but they are generally disinterested in leadership. It requires exposure and opens them up to criticism that Fours may not want to face. Their relatively low self-confidence and shyness also makes leadership difficult. They are sensitive to the rejection that leaders are subject to. Also, their independence adds to their disinterest in being a leader. They want to stand out for their uniqueness rather than for having others follow and emulate them.

When Stressed: Their decreasing confidence, increasing pessimism, and tendency to withdraw under pressure make stressed Fours poor leaders. They may also be demanding and expect special treatment—behaviors that breed hostility in followers. They fear that their tempestuous emotional reactions may get the best of them under the demands of leadership.

Influence: *wielding effective tactics for persuasion*

Typically: Fours can be passionate advocates for a cause that they believe in; they can make compelling, articulate arguments for their point of view. Their ability to be creative and self-expressive supports their talent for nuance and finding just the thing that is needed to sway an individual or group. However, their lack of self-confidence often undermines their desire to persuade others, and inhibits them from taking on influential roles. Fours are generally not seen as the visible leader influencing others toward a specific vision. Instead, they prefer to influence others in more abstract ways—though artistic expression, creative thought, or nurturing support.

When Stressed: When forced to have to influence others, stress can make Fours overly emotional, combative, dismissive, and condescending—all qualities that diminish effectiveness in influencing others. They may become easily frustrated and lose patience with people who do not see their point of view. Rather than being persuasive, stressed Fours become critical and faultfinding, making others less inclined to be influenced.

Conflict Management: *Negotiating and resolving disputes*

Typically: Self-aware Fours can use their empathy and insight to be open to resolving disputes unemotionally. They are willing to commit time and energy to exploring the dispute and trying to work out a compromise. Their high degree of empathy makes it easy for them to see the other person's point of view. Their shyness, however, sometimes makes them reluctant to being completely open. Their need to fully process their thoughts and feelings may make them hesitate to take action in conflict situations, making them appear stubborn and aloof to others.

When Stressed: Fours may become combative, unwilling to listen, refuse to compromise, and/or retreat and sulk. They can become rigid and critical, pointing out others' flaws and ignoring their own shortcomings. They become more identified with their stance and are consequently more hostile toward their opponent or more withdrawn and self-pitying, seeing themselves as misunderstood victims or martyrs.

The Awareness to Action Process

Improving Self-Confidence

Self-Confidence is an area where many Fours struggle. Unlocking the Four's full capacity for high performance often lies in improving in this competency. What follows is an example of how a Four might work on this key developmental area; it is not a literal "cook book" for all Fours, and you may find that improving performance in other competencies is more critical for you. The purpose of this example is to demonstrate how you might use the three steps of The Awareness to Action Process to identify *your* specific developmental areas and improve in those areas.

Other competencies that Fours would do well to improve in are Optimism and Adaptability. Self-Confidence, Optimism, and Adaptability are interrelated and improvement in one often facilitates improvement in the other two. Optimism involves anticipating and expecting the best possible outcome as well as the ability to continue working toward goals, despite obstacles. Adaptability is the ability to handle change and a variety of challenges without being knocked off course. Confidence in one's powers and ability supports both Optimism and Adaptability, and vice versa.

When formulating your own action plan, work on one or two important goals at a time; create small steps that will move you toward each goal; go from easiest to most difficult, and celebrate your success.

Phase One: Build Awareness
Identify a goal.

- Improve performance in the emotional competency of Self-Confidence.

Identify your current patterns.

- "I continually compare myself to people and usually see others as more talented, better equipped, better educated, etc. I struggle to fit into most work situations and am very sensitive to the judgments of others. I often feel inadequate and defective in some way."

Phase Two: Develop Authenticity

Identify how your Preferred Strategy is in conflict with improving in this competency.

- "To me, Striving to be Unique often translates into focusing on how I am different than others, which for me inevitably gets around to focusing on my shortcomings. Concentrating on being unique involves being sensitive, intuitive and, in a sense, alien. I tend to look for what's missing in me, and what needs improvement or refinement. My standards are extremely high and I judge myself by them and I seldom measure up, which is all in conflict with Self-Confidence."

Revise your strategy so that it incorporates improvement in this competence. (Remember that when Fours overdo their Striving to be Unique they may feel misunderstood and withdraw from others.)

- "True uniqueness lies in my gifts, not my weaknesses. I know I have great insight, creativity, strength, and sensitivity. By recognizing my special strengths and staying focused on the present reality rather than a disappointing past or a romanticized future, I feel a sense of confidence in who I am and what I can accomplish."

Phase Three: Take Action

Devise and Execute an Action Plan; be sure that it involves a goal, action steps, a person who will help monitor your success, and a timeline for completion. See Appendix C for a sample Action Plan. Sample action steps are listed below.

- Accept yourself as you are. Acknowledge and appreciate what you do well. As much as possible, try focusing only on your strengths and accomplishments rather than your flaws. Stop looking for what is deficient and missing in yourself and appreciate your contributions. The irony is that you want others to appreciate what you do, even while you criticize yourself.
- Set goals, and get things done. Don't wait for inspiration to strike. Have a daily schedule and stick to it.
- Keep showing up, and never give up. Even when you feel that the world is not appreciating and supporting you, get to work. Trust that the mood will shift and you will find a more positive outlook. Confidence comes from doing and accomplishing.

- Learn about the nuts and bolts of your business or company. Try not to judge the less creative, but necessary activities that keep the business running, as less important than what you do. Seeing how your activities fit within the whole of the organization is a practical way of avoiding self-absorption and becoming a team player.
- Believe in your talents and abilities. This will help motivate you to work harder and to persevere through difficulties.
- See Appendix B, General Recommendations for Growth.

CHAPTER EIGHT

TYPE FIVE:
STRIVING TO BE DETACHED

Solitude makes us tougher toward ourselves and tender toward others: in both ways it improves our character.
FRIEDRICH NIETZSCHE

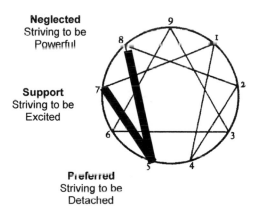

Neglected
Striving to be
Powerful

Support
Striving to be
Excited

Preferred
Striving to be
Detached

Portrait of a Five

Jack loved computers as far back as he can remember, and built his first computer from a kit when he was in junior high. "I was a hacker at six and I was programming at ten. In high school I could teach the computer science class," he will tell you. Jack was hired as a computer programmer at an insurance company in Hartford straight out of college. After only six months on the job, he was being called "the IT Wizard" because he had designed an integrated system for analyzing information that was so far superior to what competitors had that it gave the company a marked advantage over other insurance companies. Not only did the software give his company competitive advantage, it also affected other aspects of the company.

"Jack is an indispensable part of this company," his boss told us. "He has a profound grasp of our business and of what IT can do to help us be more profitable. His software innovations have been responsible for streamlining our operations so that we were able to downsize our department by 50%."

Whenever anyone has an IT question, they go to Jack. His knowledge is encyclopedic when it comes to understanding what each of his internal customers needs. The marketing department recently launched a new ad campaign in record time based on his ability to develop a program that could flawlessly track customer responses. As the marketing manager puts it, "Since Jack's been on board, I don't hesitate to take chances. I know he can back me up with the data I need to feel confident."

"He's an interesting character," we were told by a coworker. "He's immensely curious. He wants to know what the world is made of and how it operates. He's always questioning things and isn't satisfied with superficial answers. He really delves into whatever interests him, and becomes an expert in it. He analyzes everything. Sometimes I'll say hello to him and he'll walk right past me without saying a word. I used to be bothered by it, but now I just figure he's preoccupied by some idea."

One colleague, from the training department, described Jack as "Mr. Spock," after the character from Star Trek. Much like Spock, Jack is known for his superior intellect, analytical ability, and lack of emotions. "I worked with Jack to develop a training program to teach people to use one of his new programs. I wouldn't call him a people person," she remarked. "He can be impatient and a bit remote at times, and asking him to go over things more than twice can be daunting. His tone of voice can be impatient, even arrogant at times."

Jack is a Five. Of course, not all Fives have exactly the same traits that Jack does, but some of his characteristics will resonate with you if you are a Five. You may also recognize some of these behaviors if you know a Five. Jack, like all Fives, is motivated by striving to be detached.

The rest of this chapter explores the personality dynamics of Fives and shows how they can improve performance in the emotional competencies.

The Strategies

The Preferred Strategy: Striving to be Detached

Fives interact with the world by Striving to be Detached. Different Fives may use different words for "Striving to be Detached," such as wanting to be analytical, withdrawn, knowledgeable, informed, etc. Regardless of the words they use, however, Fives are observant, logical, and generally reserved. They are highly cerebral and focus on problem solving, innovative ideas, and data gathering.

When Fives overdo their Preferred Strategy, "detached" becomes distorted into "remote." Stressed Fives deal with the world by holding onto their feelings and thoughts, preferring isolation to engagement. Others may see them as distant, passionless, and lacking vitality.

The Neglected Strategy: Striving to be Powerful

The strategy at Point Eight, Striving to be Powerful, in some ways contradicts the Five's desire to be detached. Being powerful in a visible and personal way requires passion and engagement—the opposite of detachment. Therefore, Fives become uncomfortable with this strategy and "neglect" it. Rather than seeing the full value of being powerful, they distort it and see it as *being uncontrolled*. Fives may fear that if they do not remain guarded and emotionally restrained they will either become overwhelmed or their pent-up emotions will spiral out of control.

This is not to say that Fives are completely uninterested in power and influence. In fact, Fives often have a strong desire to have an impact on their environment. However, they prefer to do so quietly and from behind the scenes rather than visibly leading from the front; and they rely on intellect and strategy to influence rather than on personal forcefulness or charisma.

The Contradiction: Reserve vs. Hostility

The neglect of the natural and healthy desire to be powerful— energetic and forceful—causes the Five to act out the Neglected Strategy in subtle and predictable ways. Fives are usually reserved, but sometimes they can display hostility. For example, they can be arrogant and dismissive of the ideas of people who they believe are intellectually inferior. When Fives become aware that they are acting this way, they will quickly revert to their typical "Five-ish" behavior of being distant and aloof.

The Support Strategy: Striving to be Excited

Fives use Striving to be Excited, the strategy found at Point Seven, to reinforce being detached. They enthusiastically dive into the details of a project or problem and use their energy to spur more analysis and investigation. Fives gleefully collect information and details that others overlook, and often have great interest in obscure topics. However, they may also become distracted, forgetful, and manic when they become too absorbed in their intellectual pursuits and may become unresponsive to the more-practical demands placed on them. They may use their excitement about ideas and facts to avoid getting in touch with their emotions or connecting emotionally with other people.

Fives At Their Best

When Fives are at their best, they use all three of the strategies naturally and appropriately rather than in the habitual patterns described above. They are objective and analytical without being remote; they are assertive and proactive without being hostile or arrogant; and they are enthusiastic and engaged without being distracted and scattered.

Fives At a Glance

Examples of Fives: Bill Gates, Bobby Fisher, Jane Goodall, Alfred Hitchcock, Bob Dylan, Stephen King, Charles Darwin.

Chief Asset: *Insight.* Fives have the capacity to analyze their environment quickly and synthesize their observations into the big picture. They see things that others do not.

What They Like in Others: Intelligence, innovation, curiosity.

What They Dislike in Others: Emotional reactions, high-pressure, crowds.

How They Frustrate Others: Lack of action, intellectual arrogance, withholding of emotions.

Approach to Problem Solving: "Let's make sure we have all of the facts."

Belief About Work: "Things work best when I'm left to my own devices."

How Others See Fives: Strategic, visionary, perceptive, analytical but sometimes withdrawn, unresponsive, distant, lacking emotions.

Fives Get Into Trouble When They Tell Themselves: "I'll be safe if no one knows what I truly think or feel."

Blind Spot: *Intellectual arrogance.* Fives are often unaware of their tendency to be intellectually arrogant and the effect it has on their relationships. They spend much of their time thinking about and analyzing life, while other people spend more time actually living life. Consequently, Fives think that other people are less thoughtful and insightful and in the extreme, stupid and dull.

The Five Leader: The Strategist

The High Side of the Strategist: Fives are highly analytical and able to develop a plan for getting from current reality to identified vision.

The Low Side of the Strategist: Fives can be remote and detached and focus more on analysis than action.

Where They Shine: *At figuring things out.* Fives are great in an environment where they have the opportunity to analyze, research, innovate, and solve complex problems.

The Enneagram Emotional Competencies

As we have already discussed in Chapter Two, *emotional intelligence* is the ability to (1) identify your emotions and manage your responses to them, and (2) identify the emotions of others and manage your responses to them. The following *emotional competencies* are a set of sixteen specific capabilities based on emotional intelligence. They indicate how well Fives use emotional intelligence personally and socially.

PERSONAL COMPETENCIES

Self-Awareness

Self-Awareness: ability to identify one's thought processes, emotions, and skills
Typically: Fives are highly aware of their thought processes but tend to ignore their emotions. More than any other type, Fives identify with their intellect and they are in tune with tracking how their mind moves from one idea to another. They sometimes deny that they feel emotions, but in fact they are usually repressing and ignoring them. This can work to distort their view of themselves, leading to lowered self-awareness. They often do not trust their skills associated with action and performance, even if those skills are highly developed. They are aware of the awkwardness and anxiety that they often feel in groups.
When Stressed: Fives have a tendency to dissociate and get lost in their thoughts, becoming even more out of touch with their emotions. Their feelings, particularly anger and frustration, can rise to the surface in an uncontrolled way that affects both their thoughts and their abilities. Their thinking becomes less objective, and they may either become arrogant or isolated.

Self-Confidence: confidence in one's powers and abilities
Typically: Fives may have confidence in their areas of expertise but are generally timid when it comes to interacting with others. While they may be influential thinkers, scientists, and theorists, Fives often lack confidence in their ability to assert themselves and have an impact on their world outside of that area of expertise. They may lack the desire to venture out into the world of people and put their ideas into action. They have concerns that they will be judged to be

inadequate, and that people will put demands on them that they may not be able to meet.

When Stressed: Fives can become trapped in anxiety and insecurity. Seeing the world as dangerous and overwhelming, Fives seek the safety of their thoughts. They may become defensive and lash out as those they see as intellectually inferior but more comfortable in the world of action. As stress increases, Fives become more focused on their internal, cognitive fantasy world and can become dissociated from reality.

Self-Management

Self-Control: restraint exercised over one's impulses, emotions or desires

Typically: Their innate ability to detach from their emotions makes Fives naturals at controlling their impulses. Because they do not have a strong desire to overtly impact their environment and try to go through life fairly unnoticed, Fives tend to act with restraint. Their focus and curiosity makes them generally hardworking and able to stay with projects for long periods without being distracted by their impulses.

When Stressed: Their strong sense of autonomy may make Fives feel that rules do not apply to them and they may feel no guilt over doing whatever they want rather than focusing on the task at hand. Their emotions, such as anger, frustration, and even hostility, may also rise to the surface and make it easier to rationalize giving in to their impulses.

Adaptability: flexibility in handling change

Typically: Fives are good at improving on ideas, technologies, and products, so in this regard they are good at handling change. However, they dislike imposed change, especially if they think it is arbitrary or unnecessary. They are not necessarily wedded to policies, rules, and procedures for their own sake, so changes to these do not seem to affect Fives. However, they work hard to build their own routines and they find patterns comforting. Having their own processes and patterns allows them to spend less time thinking about things they see as inconsequential.

When Stressed: Fives may become arrogant and reject change and those who initiate it. They do this quietly, becoming stubborn and acting passive-aggressively. Rather than stand up publicly and speak out, they may withdraw and wait until events sort themselves out. If

Fives strongly oppose the change, they may quietly undermine its implementation.

Trustworthiness: *maintaining standards of honesty and integrity*
Typically: Fives tend to have high standards of honesty and integrity. They have an inner sense of perfectionism and orderliness that makes it difficult for them to be deceptive. They work to avoid conflict and emotional entanglements, so they prefer to be truthful from the beginning rather than risk complication. Their intellectual rigor predisposes them to being honest; they are dependent on facts for their security, and if the facts are wrong, their security can be threatened. Fives do, however, have a tendency to withhold. They find safety in not exposing themselves—mainly their thoughts and emotions—to others, so they may be deceptive through omission about what they are thinking or feeling.
When Stressed: Fives are motivated by an internal drive rather than the opinions of others, so they rarely have reason to lie. In fact, they often enjoy being somewhat outrageous in their opinions and insights. Interestingly, stress may cause Fives to be "brutally honest," giving them the courage to say things that they have heretofore held back. Again, however, they can be even more withholding and get themselves out of dealing with sticky situations by simply not allowing others to see their real thoughts, feelings, and motivations.

Optimism: *ability to anticipate and expect the best possible outcome*
Typically: With people they trust and in situations where they feel comfortable, Fives can have a childlike curiosity and optimism. Generally, however, Fives may struggle with optimism. They tend to be apprehensive and to look at worst-case scenarios. Their approach to life is not necessarily to embrace it but to step back from it. They often do not trust that others are benevolent, and they may see the world as dangerous.
When Stressed: Fives become even more pessimistic. They believe that the world is trying to rob them of their vitality, rather than enable them to thrive. They may feel that the world is closing in on them, and that others are taking more and more of their energy. Stressed Fives may feel small and vulnerable, and they withdraw so they will be safe.

Initiative: *readiness to act on opportunities*
Typically: Fives are quick to act on opportunities to explore ideas and to present their ideas to others. They may struggle, however, with implementing those ideas on a practical level. Implementation is

difficult for Fives for two reasons: first, they find ideas more interesting than action; second, they tend to be set back easily by criticism and obstacles. In general, while Fives may be creative and innovative, they tend to be collectors of data who would prefer to hand the data to others who can then act upon it.

When Stressed: Their tendency to withdraw and to go into their thoughts makes it difficult for Fives to show initiative. They lose their desire to act and prefer to sit on the sidelines and observe. Highly stressed Fives can become almost paralyzed by indecision and unwillingness to act.

Achievement Drive: striving to meet or improve a standard of excellence

Typically: Fives have a powerful drive to prove their intelligence and to meet or exceed intellectual standards. However, they tend to be disinterested in standard measures of achievement. They are motivated to pursue their own intellectual curiosities and may get satisfaction out of finding answers and approaches to problem solving that others may miss. They are concerned more with process than with accomplishment, so they are less concerned with the outside pressures that may motivate other types to achieve. More than most other types, Fives march to the beat of their own drummers and are often indifferent to the opinions of other people.

When Stressed: Fives withdraw and may become completely indifferent to achievement. They may feel resigned to the idea that their interests and skills are not appreciated or understood by others and are not rewarded in the corporate world. Stressed Fives may achieve just enough to keep their jobs while pursuing their real interests on the side.

Resiliency: capacity to endure in the face of obstacles

Typically: If Fives can use their ability to detach, they do not take obstacles too seriously, and therefore endure them fairly well. In fact, self-aware Fives may actually enjoy obstacles to their intellectual pursuits because there is more satisfaction in solving a difficult problem than a simple one. Fives address obstacles to action by observing and studying them, but tend not to get emotionally affected by them. They will pick the obstacle apart and tackle it in digestible pieces rather than trying to smash through barriers.

When Stressed: If possible, Fives will find comfort in simply ignoring the problem and hoping that others resolve it. If forced to face it, Fives may develop a nervous energy in the face of obstacles and go into their heads and become obsessive in their efforts to figure out the problem. They experience anxiety and may refuse to ask for help.

SOCIAL COMPETENCIES

Attunement to Others

Empathy: awareness of and participation in others' feelings, ideas, and needs
Typically: Fives connect with others through ideas rather than emotions. They enjoy finding common ground through thoughts rather than experiences. Though not openly emotional, Fives can be sensitive and caring and willing to lend a hand to those they see in need. However, they may struggle with showing empathy with others' feelings. Fives can be uncomfortable with their own feelings and even more awkward trying to relate to other people's emotional issues.
When Stressed: Their pattern of withdrawing from others when under stress makes it difficult for Fives to be empathic. In fact, the more stressed they are, the more they try to avoid and ignore other people's emotions. Stress causes Fives to shut out the world rather than participate in it.

Political Awareness: reading a group's emotional currents and power relationships
Typically: Fives generally do not have much interest in emotions, but they are keen observers of politics. They enjoy sitting on the outskirts and dispassionately watching how people interact. They like having power but prefer being powerful from behind the scenes to sitting on the throne of power. Because they often feel uninvolved in the goings on around them, they make excellent impartial students of how people behave. However, many Fives do not read emotional currents well. They work hard to repress their own emotions and are uncomfortable with those of others; thus, they are less familiar with emotions than most other types and may be less adept at reading them.
When Stressed: Again, Fives simply disengage and become uninterested in office politics. This can work to their detriment. It makes it more difficult to utilize an organization's resources and to get support for their projects or ideas. Their lack of interest in reading emotional currents also makes it more difficult for Fives to connect with others, thus making it more difficult to make their own projects come to fruition.

Communication: *listening openly and sending convincing messages*
Typically: Fives are often reluctant to initiate conversations in social settings, preferring that others speak while they listen. They often feel that their interests will not be interesting to others. Once they feel comfortable, however, they will talk at length on topics of common interest. They communicate factually and with great insight. Fives have a desire to be understood and enjoy sharing their knowledge, and they can generate excitement around topics they are enthusiastic about. They sometimes run the risk of being too abstract and long-winded and neglecting to show their feelings about what they are discussing. They tend to be attentive listeners if the topic is of interest to them, but Fives may be obviously inattentive otherwise.
When Stressed: Fives may become intellectually arrogant and talk down to people who they believe are not as intelligent as they are. The more stressed they become, the less they share their feelings. Under significant stress they simply do not communicate. They may withdraw and ignore others, seeming disinterested and distant.

Relationship Building

Cooperation: *working with others toward shared goals*
Typically: Fives often make better individual contributors than team players. Fives are highly autonomous and do not like having to move at the pace of others, whether they view it as too fast or too slow. They like the opportunity to pursue their own ideas and may see teams as an unnecessary burden. They also may struggle with bonding with others and often feel like outsiders, even with people with whom they have worked for many years. Fives often do not trust that others will be as thorough and rigorous as they are. They may become frustrated if people are not as well prepared for a project, as the Five believes they should be.
When Stressed: Fives struggle with cooperation. They tend to neglect communicating their needs, actions, or abilities to others, so they may neither benefit from the team nor enhance it. Their timidity may make them feel like outsiders and they may be viewed as such by others on the team. They are often unconsciously intimidating to others who may not know how to interpret Fives' mixture of intelligence and distance.

Leadership: *inspiring and leading individuals and groups*
Typically: Fives are generally disinterested in the passion and emotional investment that leadership requires. Because they find

leadership to be too much of a drain to their reservoir of vital energy, Fives hesitate to expose themselves to the scrutiny and possible embarrassment brought on by the demands of leadership. Leadership involves quick decision-making and resolving interpersonal disputes, areas where Fives may struggle.

When Stressed: Fives lose interest in leadership and may abdicate their responsibilities. They may see leadership as a burden rather than an opportunity and may disengage from those who depend on them. While they may be experts in their field, their lack of apparent enthusiasm and emotion makes it difficult for others to rally around stressed Fives.

Influence: wielding effective tactics for persuasion
Typically: Fives persuade others by relying on data and facts, rather than on passion and inspiration. Their mastery of a topic and their ability to articulate it are an asset in swaying others to their way of thinking. Others often look to Fives for advice and guidance. Because they are so insightful, Fives also enjoy persuading people from behind the scenes, influencing with a well-placed comment or observation.

When Stressed: If a rational presentation of the facts does not work, Fives who are invested in an outcome will resort to displays of anger and arrogance to persuade others. Stressed Fives, because of their intellectual arrogance, do not respond very well when others do not listen to their point of view. If they are not invested in the outcome, however, stressed Fives may simply walk away.

Conflict Management: Negotiating and resolving disputes
Typically: Fives are usually able to stay unemotional about conflict and their detachment works to their benefit in this competency. However, they are usually uncomfortable with the emotional reactions generally found in conflicts. Other people may find Fives' lack of emotional response frustrating and interpret it as a sign of disinterest, arrogance, or unwillingness to engage and work towards an agreement.

When Stressed: Fives tend to flee from conflict. Emotional conflict can be overwhelming to stressed Fives and they not only withdraw into their heads but also physically withdraw from the source of conflict. Highly stressed Fives may literally leave the room and find a refuge.

The Awareness to Action Process

Improving Communication

Communication is an area where many Fives struggle. Unlocking the Five's full capacity for high performance often lies in improving in this competency. What follows is an example of how a Five might work on this key developmental area; it is not a literal "cook book" for all Fives, and you may find that improving performance in other competencies is more critical for you. The purpose of this example is to demonstrate how you might use the three steps of The Awareness to Action Process to identify *your* specific developmental areas and improve in those areas.

Other competencies that Fives would do well to improve in are Conflict Management and Initiative. Communication, Conflict Management, and Initiative are interrelated and improvement in one often facilitates improvement in the other two. Communication involves listening openly and sending convincing messages, dealing with problems directly, sharing information, and being open to information from others. Conflict Management involves listening, asking questions, and encouraging debate and discussion. Initiative, the readiness to act on opportunities, means exploring ideas and presenting those ideas to others. Without strong communication skills, resolving disputes and implementing new initiatives are virtually impossible.

When formulating your own action plan, work on one or two important goals at a time; create small steps that will move you toward each goal; go from easiest to most difficult, and celebrate your success.

Phase One: Build Awareness
Identify a goal.
- Improve performance in the emotional competency of Communication.

Identify your current patterns.
- "I usually hesitate to start conversations, especially in social situations. I'd rather listen than talk, and feel that a lot of people are not interested in what interests me. When I find someone with a common interest I can talk incessantly, and have been accused of sounding like a 'know-it-all' and being a poor listener."

Phase Two: Develop Authenticity

Identify how your Preferred Strategy is in conflict with improving in this competency.

- "To me, Striving to be Detached often means avoiding communicating with others, preferring instead to stay with my own thoughts. I'm also not comfortable expressing or talking about my feelings. I'd rather be factual, non-emotional, and quiet than engaged in small talk and mundane conversations. When I'm impatient with people, my words may contain a condescending and intellectually arrogant quality."

Revise your strategy so that it incorporates improvement in this competency. (Remember that when Fives overdo their Striving to be Detached they might become remote and disengaged.)

- "Learning to communicate my own needs, engaging with people and resolving conflicts rather than ignoring them, helps me to find the healthy detachment, autonomy, and serenity that I desire."

Phase Three: Take Action

Devise and Execute an Action Plan; be sure that it involves a goal, action steps, a person who will help monitor your success, and a timeline for completion. See Appendix C for a sample Action Plan. Sample action steps are listed below.

- Make contact. Set a goal every day to call, e-mail, or write to a specific number of people. Don't put it off. Make contact, and *return your phone calls.*
- Study your communication style: the words you use, your tone of voice, and your body language. Be sure to make eye contact.
- Don't interrupt or zone out. Listen to other people's perspective. You don't have to agree with them, but be patient and allow people to express their ideas.
- Eliminate judgmental, intellectually arrogant expressions such as, "The reality of the situation is…" and "You don't seem to understand."
- Communicate in practical rather than abstract language. Check to see that what you are offering is useful and relevant, and not simply a way for you to show how much you know. Offer information, theories and ideas that your colleagues can use, and *get to the point.* Most

people don't have a desire to know as many details as you do.

- See Appendix B, General Recommendations for Growth.

CHAPTER NINE

TYPE SIX: *STRIVING TO BE SECURE*

Security is stability within ourselves.
BERNARD BARUCH

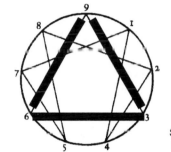

Neglected
Striving to be
Peaceful

Preferred
Striving to be
Secure

Support
Striving to be
Outstanding

Portrait of a Six

Tim is a corporate trainer for a pharmaceutical company. He travels extensively presenting workshops on FDA Regulations for New Drug Applications. His latest trip will take him to Stuttgart, Munich, and Hamburg. Tim has been prepared for this trip for weeks. He's been packed, his Power Point presentation is ready, his participant guidebooks have been shipped and delivered to the workshop site, and all the participants have been contacted. Nothing has been overlooked. "When I feel secure that everything will go well, I can relax. I can focus on my presentation, rather than worry about the logistics," he told us. "I'm an expert at handling anxiety. I have a way of looking into the future, anticipating what might go wrong, and preparing for it." And he adds with a smile, "I was a boy scout as a kid, and I still follow the scout motto: 'Be Prepared.' "

"He's the glue that holds our team together," said Tim's boss. "No one is as quick to roll up his sleeves and get to work as Tim. I've seen him sacrifice many an evening and weekend out of a sense of responsibility to the team. And he'll do it with little need of personal recognition." Tim is acknowledged by his peers to be a perfect co-trainer, able to pass the baton to his partner easily and without ego issues.

Tim responds well to crises thrown his way. When he and a colleague planned to drive from Philadelphia to Washington, DC to conduct a two-day workshop, a major accident shut down the interstate. The delay would have caused them to miss the morning of the workshop, but Tim had mapped alternative routes to the site for just such an emergency. They were able to get off the interstate and still make it to the workshop in time.

Tim has the ability to accurately assess the motivations and relative positions of others. However, his coworkers point out that sometimes he is too suspicious—attributing malicious intent where there is none. He can also be pessimistic, negative, skeptical, and cynical.

"He can drive you crazy in planning meetings," said a colleague. "The group will be excited about an idea and we'll be on a roll about a new way of developing a module or responding to a customer, and Tim will jump in with, 'Have you thought about what might happen if . . . ? It deflates the whole team and forces us to focus on failure. While the rest of us were brainstorming fabulous ideas, he was anticipating catastrophes. He makes us look at all the contingencies. To be honest, though, he improves our planning process. We can go forward with a more realistic point of view."

Tim's cautious nature has its good and bad sides. "I take a defensive stance—both physically and mentally—quite naturally. I'm hard-wired for defense. I can sniff out trouble, unsafe proposals, people, and deals."

Tim is a Six. Of course, not all Sixes have exactly the same traits that Tim does, but some of his characteristics will resonate with you if you are a Six. You may also recognize some of these behaviors if you know a Six. Tim, like all Sixes, is motivated by striving to be secure.

The rest of this chapter explores the personality dynamics of Sixes and shows how they can improve performance in the emotional competencies.

The Strategies

The Preferred Strategy: Striving to be Secure

Sixes interact with the world by Striving to be Secure. Different Sixes may use different words for "Striving to be Secure," such as wanting to be vigilant, dutiful, careful, accepted by the group, etc. Regardless of the words they use, however, Sixes are careful, responsible, and protective of the welfare of the group. They focus on maintaining consistency, tradition, and team cohesion. They are prepared for emergencies and able to see through weak arguments and deceptive logic.

When Sixes overdo their Preferred Strategy, "security" becomes distorted into "mediocrity." Stressed Sixes deal with the world by being conservative and unwilling to take the risks that are sometimes necessary for high achievement. They are not comfortable trusting their own judgment and can become fearful, suspicious, bureaucratic, and uncooperative.

The Neglected Strategy: Striving to be Peaceful

The strategy at Point Nine, Striving to be Peaceful, in some ways contradicts the Six's desire to be secure. Sixes find comfort in the constant vigilance of scanning their environment for danger, making the calm and relaxed approach of the Nine undesirable. Therefore, Sixes become uncomfortable with this strategy and "neglect" it. Rather than seeing the full value of Striving to be Peaceful, Sixes distort it and see it as *passivity*. They fear that if they relax their guard they will be vulnerable to unseen dangers.

This is not to say that Sixes are incapable of creating an atmosphere of peacefulness and calm. In fact, creating this sort of environment for others is a high priority for Sixes. Their vigilance in spotting problems and being prepared for what could go wrong often allows others to relax and feel safe, a luxury that Sixes rarely allow themselves.

The Contradiction: Responsibility vs. Laziness

The neglect of the natural and healthy need for peacefulness causes Sixes to act out the Neglected Strategy in subtle and predictable ways. Sixes are usually responsible, but sometimes they may become lazy.

For example, they may leave simple tasks undone or expect others to do a job for which the Six is responsible. When they become aware that they are acting this way they will quickly revert to their typical "Six-ish" behavior of being anxiously productive.

The Support Strategy: Striving to be Outstanding

Sixes use Striving to be Outstanding, the strategy found at Point Three, to reinforce being secure. While perhaps never really trusting their abilities, Sixes know that expertise in a particular area—and making sure that others notice that expertise—will be to their benefit. Their drive to be accomplished, conscientious, and dutiful workers creates security by highlighting their value to the group. However, under stress they may become overly concerned with pointing out their achievements—and the shortcomings of others—in an effort to gain security.

Sixes At Their Best

When Sixes are at their best, they use all three strategies naturally and appropriately rather than in the habitual patterns described above. They create safety and security for themselves and others without being fearful and suspicious; they are relaxed and calm without shirking their responsibilities; and they are accomplished without feeling the need to make everyone aware of their achievements.

Sixes At a Glance

Examples of Sixes: George H.W. Bush, Meg Ryan, Jon Stewart, Woody Allen, Ellen DeGeneres, J. Edgar Hoover, Mel Gibson.

Chief Asset: *Support.* Sixes are steadfast, responsible, and dependable. They are determined to perform their duty, to do what is best for the group, and provide for the needs of others.

What They Like in Others: Dependability, support/protectiveness, hard work.

What They Dislike in Others: Ambiguity, undependability, deviance (from the norms of group).

How They Frustrate Others: Complaining, indecision, lack of trust.

Approach to Problem Solving: "I need to find out what else can go wrong and who I can depend on."

Belief About Work: "Things work best when I know everyone's agenda."

How Others See Sixes: Engaging, upbeat, team-oriented, caring, but sometimes anxious, suspicious, combative, and fearful.

Sixes Get Into Trouble When They Tell Themselves: "Someone else represents an idealized authority that I can either cling to or rebel against."

Blind Spot: *Complaining.* Sixes are often unaware of their tendency to complain and its affect on their relationships. Because Sixes do not trust their own thought process they are constantly trying to gauge other people's reactions (to test the waters) to a given stimulus to see if there is a threat that needs attention. They complain to see if people agree or disagree with them as a way of finding where people stand.

The Six Leader: The Guardian

The High Side of the Guardian: Sixes identify internal and external threats to the organization, and protect group cohesion.

The Low Side of the Guardian: Sixes can be fearful and suspicious, focusing on what could go wrong rather than what could go right.

Where They Shine: *Anticipating problems.* Sixes thrive in situations where they have the opportunity to play Devil's Advocate and prepare the team for potential difficulties.

The Enneagram Emotional Competencies

As we have already discussed in Chapter Two, *emotional intelligence* is the ability to (1) identify your emotions and manage your responses to them, and (2) identify the emotions of others and manage your responses to them. The following *emotional competencies* are a set of sixteen specific capabilities based on emotional intelligence. They indicate how well Sixes use emotional intelligence personally and socially.

PERSONAL COMPETENCIES

Self-Awareness

Self-Awareness: ability to identify one's thought processes, emotions, and skills
Typically: Sixes are keen observers of both their external and internal world and tend to be highly aware of their thought processes, emotions, and skills. A major focus of the Six is understanding how they fit into the group, so they constantly check in on themselves and try to make sure they are in alignment with those whose opinions they value. The problem they often run into, however, is that they do not trust their own thoughts, feelings, or actions. They may make a decision and then question it. They may identify a thought or emotion and then question whether it is the correct one to have. This questioning may make them seem, even to themselves, to be less self-aware than they really are.
When Stressed: Sixes' anxiety makes it difficult for them to clearly identify their thoughts, feelings, or emotions. Once they think they have pinned them down, they question themselves and wonder if they are actually experiencing the opposite. Stressed Sixes can become confused about what they really think or feel. In an attempt to escape the resulting anxieties, they lose themselves in busywork.

Self-Confidence: confidence in one's powers and abilities
Typically: In areas that they have worked hard to develop, Sixes can have a fairly high degree of self-confidence. They tend to carve out a niche for themselves—such as a job, a sport or a hobby—where they feel safe and confident. Outside of that niche, however, they struggle with this competency. Sixes will still doubt themselves in other areas of their lives. They may feel that they are lacking in internal powers

and abilities, and they turn outward for support and guidance. They may appear to be unsure of themselves, to be indecisive, and to vacillate—behavior that is based on their belief that the world is not a safe place. At the same time, they may be slow to ask for help because they do not want to admit that they rely on others for their security.

When Stressed: Sixes may begin to doubt themselves even more and become increasingly indecisive. They may obsess over whether they can accomplish the tasks they are responsible for and begin to fear failure more and more. As stress increases, Sixes may imagine ordinary activities turning into disasters. They may begin to rely more on other people, procedures, or belief systems. Highly stressed Sixes become increasingly suspicious that things will go wrong and that people are against them. Some Sixes under stress may take on an air of bravado and become highly aggressive as a way to hide their anxiety.

Self-Management

Self-Control: restraint exercised over one's impulses, emotions or desires

Typically: This is a strong competency for Sixes, who are very conscious of the expectations of their environment and diligent in meeting those expectations. They prefer to play it safe and to be conservative: Controlling their impulses helps create a steady, and therefore secure, home base for Sixes. Self-control is a way for Sixes to show how responsible they are, and that they can be depended on. Working hard to control what they think, feel, and do allows Sixes to feel more relaxed and secure. Sixes are often most in control in times of crisis. Crises, therefore, can often clear their heads, help their doubts disappear, and show them the action to take so they can move courageously. They can restrain their fears and anxieties and can be decisive, no-nonsense leaders.

When Stressed: Sixes can become rigid and unbending. They cling to rules and procedures and may frustrate others with their unwillingness to be flexible. At the same time, stress causes Sixes to become more fearful, and their fear may cause them to let their impulses and emotions run wild. They may construct unrealistic worst-case scenarios, become combative, or give in to anxiety that makes it difficult for them to take effective action.

Adaptability: flexibility in handling change
Typically: Self-aware Sixes can adapt to change easily. As long as they receive a clear message from a trusted leader or group, they can leverage their ability and desire to believe in a person, cause, or vision, and can change directions more easily. Less-aware Sixes struggle with adapting to change. They like the traditional, and change creates anxiety for them. One of their first reactions to change is to feel threatened and to doubt that they will have adequate support to manage. When Sixes find something they can trust and feel secure with, they do not want to alter it. Sixes often feel they cannot trust what they do not know.

When Stressed: Sixes may tend to be suspicious of deviations from the norm and may see sinister plots behind change efforts. Anxiety increases and they can react in different ways. They may become rigid and combative toward the source of change. They may also take a more phobic response and panic or become overwhelmed by their anxiety; they may act impulsively in an attempt to bring some resolution to their anxieties and to re-establish a sense of normalcy and security.

Trustworthiness: maintaining standards of honesty and integrity
Typically: Their desire for certainty makes most Sixes place a high value on honesty. Honesty and integrity translate to consistency, and consistency is what Sixes seek. They have a very highly developed work ethic and put in long hours to demonstrate their worth and loyalty. They are guardians of company and personal values and believe in idealism and tradition. Self-aware Sixes are probably the most dependable and trustworthy of all the types. They are assertive and dutiful in their pursuit of honesty and integrity.

When Stressed: Stress does not make Sixes any less honest, but it makes them more rigid about fulfilling their commitments. For example, their desire to make sure that they are on time for a meeting may cause them to show up an hour early. They may become argumentative, aggressive, and staunch defenders of standards. As stress increases, they may project their flaws onto others as a way of guarding against being seen as flawed themselves. This is a form of dishonesty in that it takes the focus off of them and puts it onto others, sometimes undeservedly.

Optimism: ability to anticipate and expect the best possible outcome
Typically: In general, Sixes tend to be more pessimistic than optimistic. Their focus is on danger and the things that could go wrong, rather than on opportunity and the things that could go right.

Authority is a major factor in the thinking and behavior of Sixes. Self-aware Sixes can be optimistic if an authority they trust is at the helm of a project. Their sense of optimism stems from their faith and loyalty in this person. While this predisposition makes them struggle in this competency, Sixes provide a valuable service to organizations by sniffing out potential problems that others miss. They often play the much-needed role of Devil's Advocate.

When Stressed: Sixes may become skeptical, cynical, and chronically uncertain. Their lack of self-confidence under stress exacerbates their tendency to see things negatively. Rather than focusing on opportunities and anticipating positive outcomes, their view becomes negative and they see danger lurking behind every corner.

Initiative: readiness to act on opportunities
Typically: In general, Sixes are conservative and hesitant to take risks. While they may see opportunity when it arises, their tendency to second guess often gets in the way of their acting on it. If they feel that they have proper support and that their group is behind them, they are ready to act on opportunities. If they do not feel that they have that support, however, they will be more reluctant. Sixes generally spend a lot of time building consensus among the people whose opinions they value before taking action.

When Stressed: Sixes generally leave initiative to others. They stick with processes that worked in the past and may miss out on an opportunity if the opportunity requires a new way of doing things. Stressed Sixes are often excellent in support roles but are hesitant to take initiatives that are not explicitly described by an authority.

Achievement Drive: striving to meet or improve a standard of excellence
Typically: Accomplishment leads to a sense of security for Sixes, so self-aware Sixes can be high in this competency. Their achievement drive has an idealistic quality to it, characterized by a desire to be responsible, to meet and improve standards, and to contribute to the welfare of their family, their way of life, and their group. They may use continual improvement as a way of controlling or alleviating potentially dangerous or unpredictable events.

When Stressed: Sixes may work harder to achieve, but their anxiety may undermine their effectiveness. They can fall into a cycle of either increasing anxiety and criticizing themselves for not achieving more or blaming others for impeding their achievement. If they feel that striving after achievement will threaten their secure position, they will avoid acting, preferring the safety of conformity, often lapsing into disgruntled complaining. For example, if mediocrity is what their group expects, stressed Sixes will settle for mediocrity in an effort to fit in.

Resiliency: capacity to endure in the face of obstacles
Typically: Because Sixes have a tendency to anticipate danger and to plan for disaster, they handle obstacles fairly well. It is rare that Sixes encounter an obstacle that they have not already created a plan for resolving. They may also believe that things will be much worse than anticipated. In a strange way, the Six's habit of worrying about what disaster may befall them next prepares them for the unpredictable and increases resilience. Self-aware Sixes seem to gain power and clarity when the going gets tough. They are able to be strong emotionally, to be logical and rational, to make and trust in their own decisions and to help others through obstacles.
When Stressed: Sixes may become almost frantic about the anticipation of obstacles. They see challenges that may not exist and thus make their task more difficult. This impedes their efficiency because rather than focusing on the task at hand, they are focused on all the possible dangers that can occur.

SOCIAL COMPETENCIES

Attunement to Others

Empathy: awareness of and participation in others' feelings, ideas, and needs
Typically: Sixes are generally on the lookout for like-minded people who can be trusted and relied on. Aware of and reactive to other people, they are attuned to what others are thinking and feeling. They enjoy meeting other people's needs and proving their friendship and dependability. They like to evaluate people and actively seek a deeper understanding of their feelings, ideas, and needs. This helps them predict the behavior of others and to judge whether they can be trusted. Unless Sixes have established a friendly relationship with others, they are more interested in awareness of, rather than participation in, a person's feelings, ideas, and needs.
When Stressed: As anxiety rises, Sixes may become suspicious of others and more focused on their own needs and vulnerabilities than on the needs of others. Increased stress tends to make Sixes paranoid and they see those outside of a tight group of trusted people as

potential enemies. They will be less willing to participate in others' feelings, ideas and needs when they view them this way.

Political Awareness: *reading a group's emotional currents and power relationships*
Typically: Sixes' vigilance in scanning their environment for potential problems makes them very good at political awareness. Sixes focus on how they fit into a group, who can provide security, and where the threats are. They sense intuitively who can be trusted and who is a potential ally or enemy. Understanding the emotional currents and power relationships enables Sixes to feel comfortable and to relax their guard a little bit. Their honesty and integrity, their friendliness and good humor helps them to be trusted by others. Sixes are also excellent judges of character, especially when it comes to spotting frauds and con artists.
When Stressed: Their suspicion can make Sixes misread their environment. They may start to resent and question authority and rebel against it. They can become paranoid and defensive and project their own shortcomings onto those outside the approved-of group. Defensiveness and rigidity around their beliefs or opinions distorts the stressed Sixes' awareness of real political relationships.

Communication: *listening openly and sending convincing messages*
Typically: Sixes are often charming and engaging, and they can be excellent communicators. They are genuinely curious and want to hear what people have to say. They are positively reactive and respond to what people say to them, making the speaker feel important and appreciated. Sixes often have a sense of humor and playfulness and can be witty conversationalists. They are intelligent listeners and troubleshooters and can analyze ideas for their strengths and weaknesses very effectively. Because their communication is based on such thorough analysis, self-aware Sixes send valuable, convincing messages.
When Stressed: Anxiety keeps Sixes from sharing as much as they could. Their suspicion affects how they listen to other people. Stressed Sixes are constantly questioning the content of what people are saying, and are often thinking of counter arguments. As stress increases, they may see only the negative—problems, complications, and potential failures—and can throw a blanket of cynicism and pessimism over workable ideas.

Relationship Building

Cooperation: *working with others toward shared goals*
Typically: Sixes are generally great at cooperating with others and working toward shared goals. Their personality is structured around fitting in with the group, and they find their safety and security in building bonds based on similar values, beliefs, backgrounds, and so forth. They are constantly looking for commonality, and shared goals are the perfect way to mobilize Sixes. Sixes are also very interested in protecting other team members. They strive to maintain a high level of loyalty and respect for others, and of course, expect the same in return.
When Stressed: The group takes on a central role for most Sixes. They seek security in the approved-of group and become reluctant to do anything that will endanger their position. They become overly dependent on the group and idealize it, seeking things that the group may not be able to supply. Stressed Sixes lose their ability to trust their own decisions and may relinquish their responsibility to others. Some Sixes tend to struggle with cooperation when stressed and may be anti-authoritarian and anti-group. They may seek safety in rebellion rather than conformity.

Leadership: *inspiring and leading individuals and groups*
Typically: Sixes are generally reluctant to take leadership roles, preferring to provide support. When in leadership roles, however, they genuinely want the best for others and enjoy taking a protective and nurturing role. Six leaders can be inspiring spokespersons for the team's causes, beliefs, or values. They lead by consensus, guiding the group to establish and maintain its own values, leadership, and decision-making. They inspire by including others, being open to what the rank and file has to say, and by ensuring that the group's values, beliefs, and dreams are honored.
When Stressed: Sixes may demonstrate a fear of change and moving forward, and their caution may affect their ability to give clear guidance. They may fall back on the traditional way of doing things, and be defenders of the status quo. Stressed Sixes may feel that others are incompetent and lack the commitment that they themselves demonstrate. They may also suspect that others are trying to undermine their authority and spend more time trying to catch people in the act than in leading them. Highly stressed Sixes can be paranoid and dictatorial leaders.

Influence: wielding effective tactics for persuasion
Typically: Sixes are not easily sold on anything, so if they are convinced about something, they can be enthusiastic and zealous salespersons. They can also be relentless and dogged in their efforts to convince others of what they believe. Sixes can be masterful networkers and politically savvy. They build bonds easily and can sense the correct people to make mutually beneficial deals with. Sixes understand that "one hand washes the other" and value alliances as ways of getting things done and getting their message heard.

When Stressed: Sixes may adopt a "true-believer" mentality and become overly zealous in their attempts to persuade. They may take rejection very personally and see it as a direct challenge to their beliefs, making them even more dogmatic and aggressive in their attempts to persuade. Stressed Sixes may think that they alone know the right way, and they can become grandiose about their cause or idea and pressure others to conform to their way of thinking.

Conflict Management: Negotiating and resolving disputes
Typically: Self-aware Sixes are able to see clearly what went wrong, take responsibility for their part in the conflict without being defensive, and work toward a positive resolution. However, many Sixes may overreact to conflict, becoming overly fearful or overly aggressive. Sixes may see relatively minor conflict as something threatening, as a breakdown in the smooth operation of the relationship or system. Because alignment with the group is so important, they see disagreement as a sign that the other is attacking them, and may feel that the conflict is much worse than it is. They may focus on what can go wrong in the negotiation process and tend to miss the more hopeful aspects and growth potential that conflict can provide.

When Stressed: Sixes may see the other person as representative of an entire group—namely those who disagree with the Six. They may stereotype and give in to prejudices such as "All salespeople are alike." Stressed Sixes may feel like those who see things differently are "out to get you." They are not very good at negotiating when under stress because they tend to set up "us versus them" situations, rather than seeking win-win solutions.

The Awareness to Action Process

Improving Adaptability

Adaptability is an area where many Sixes struggle. Unlocking the Six's full capacity for high performance often lies in improving in this competency. What follows is an example of how a Six might work on this key developmental area; it is not a literal "cook book" for all Sixes, and you may find that improving performance in other competencies is more critical for you. The purpose of this example is to demonstrate how you might use the three steps of The Awareness to Action Process to identify *your* specific developmental areas and improve in those areas.

Other competencies that Sixes would do well to improve in are Optimism and Self-Confidence. Adaptability, Optimism, and Self-confidence are interrelated and improvement in one often facilitates improvement in the other two. Optimism, the ability to anticipate and expect the best possible outcome becomes easier for Sixes when they develop flexibility in handling change. Self-Confidence supports Adaptability as Sixes become more successful in adjusting their reactions and being sure enough of themselves to make quick, decisive changes.

When formulating your own action plan, work on one or two important goals at a time; create small steps that will move you toward each goal; go from easiest to most difficult, and celebrate your success.

Phase One: Build Awareness
Identify a goal.
- Improve performance in the emotional competency of Adaptability.

Identify your current behaviors.
- "I tend to avoid taking chances on anything new because I focus on danger and the things that could go wrong. I am often suspicious and skeptical that people can be completely trusted. I prefer the 'devil I know to the devil I don't'—that is, even if circumstances are not perfect, I would rather keep things the same than face the possibility that things could get worse. I need a guarantee

that things will turn out OK or I won't take the risk of embracing change. "

Phase Two: Develop Authenticity

Identify how your Preferred Strategy is in conflict with improving in this competency.

- "To me, Striving to be Secure means avoiding risks, being extremely vigilant when dealing with anything new or unknown. It involves being skeptical about adapting to shifting priorities and rapid change, all of which are in conflict with the competency of Adaptability.

Revise your strategy so that it incorporates improvement in this competency. (Remember that when Sixes overdo their Striving to be Secure they may fail to take the risks necessary for high performance and settle for mediocrity.)

- "True security involves taking necessary and appropriate risks that ensure that I will be successful. Being resistant, negative, and combative when change is called for may make me a liability to the team. Not being adaptable is unwise, ineffective, and ultimately threatens my security."

Phase Three: Take Action

Devise and Execute an Action Plan; be sure that it involves a goal, action steps, a person who will help monitor your success, and a timeline for completion. See Appendix C for a sample Action Plan. Sample action steps are listed below.

- Move out of your comfort zone. Different people, places, and events are not of themselves threatening but are often the source of security, support, and comfort.
- Recognize the high cost you pay when your actions, thoughts, or behaviors are grounded in doubt and fear of change. Beware of clinging to the traditional way of doing things when new methods or procedures are better. Placing too much trust in what used to work may place you at the greatest risk of all.
- Practice recognizing the opportunities that come with change—the positive aspects—as well as the negative. Try to gain an objective, balanced perspective on adapting your behavior.

- Stop over-analyzing, imagining the worst, procrastinate-ing, and being defensive. Take action and savor your accomplishment.
- See Appendix B, General Recommendations for Growth.

CHAPTER TEN

TYPE SEVEN:
STRIVING TO BE EXCITED

*There often seems to be a playfulness to wise people…and they can
persuade other people who are in a state of agitation to calm down
and manage a smile.*
EDWARD HOAGLAND

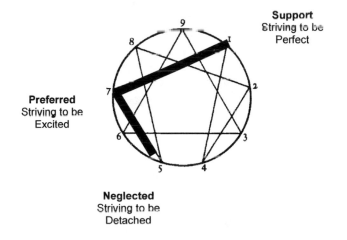

Support
Striving to be
Perfect

Preferred
Striving to be
Excited

Neglected
Striving to be
Detached

Portrait of a Seven

Jim is a partner in an investment company that specializes in
retirement plans. He is vice president of branch development, and his
job is to recruit, hire, and develop successful account representatives.
He likes what he does. "I get to meet different people every day.
Some of them are fresh out of college and have never sold anything;
others are seasoned professionals. It doesn't matter how much
experience they have. I can pick the good salespeople out of a crowd
every time."

Jim's high energy is contagious. He looks at the bright side of
things and seldom entertains the negative. "Life's too short," he'll tell
you, with a smile that lights up the room. "I believe in being happy—
plain and simple. We weren't put here to be miserable." Jim's
philosophy extends to all aspects of his life, especially work. "I don't
believe in working at a job that makes you unhappy or that's
unfulfilling. I guess I'm lucky, because I love my job. I train my reps

to help people plan their future, to make sure that their retirements are secure so that they can enjoy their senior years. But me?" he adds, "I'll never retire. I'm having too much fun."

One of Jim's partner calls him the "idea man," because, as he puts it, "he's always thinking. He's coming up with ideas at lunch, on the tennis court, in the shower. As a matter of fact, one of his ideas was a water-proof pen and pad so he could write down his ideas in the shower."

Jim has been in his present job for eight years—the longest he's stayed with one company. He's been involved in starting five businesses. They were all fun at first, but over time he grew bored. He loves the start-up aspect of new businesses, but once the newness wears off he finds his mind drifting to more exciting ventures. The routine, lackluster activities of operating a business hold little interest for him. It's the exciting aspects of an endeavor that keep him moving, motivated, and positive. That's why he likes his present job. "Hiring and developing people is something different every day. There's always new people and new experiences."

Jim runs into difficulty, however, when others do not share his enthusiasm and optimism. For example, a few years ago, he has lobbying hard to open a new office in San Francisco when the company had just opened one in Boston, and was struggling to make ends meet. "He pitched this idea to us for six months, relentlessly, with only raw enthusiasm on his side," said one of his partners. "The rest of the partners thought he was unrealistic and reckless. The harder he pushed, the more we saw what a lousy team player he was being. Jim, on the other hand, saw us as uninspired, risk-averse, and pessimistic. We worked it out, but it put a strain on the relationship."

Jim is a Seven. Of course, not all Sevens have exactly the same traits that Jim does, but some of his characteristics will resonate with you if you are a Seven. You may also recognize some of these behaviors if you know a Seven. Jim, like all Sevens, is motivated by striving to be excited.

The rest of this chapter explores the personality dynamics of Sevens and shows how they can improve performance in the emotional competencies.

The Strategies

The Preferred Strategy: Striving to be Excited

Sevens interact with the world by Striving to be Excited. Different Sevens may use different words for "Striving to be Excited," such as wanting to be happy, enthusiastic, entertaining, active, etc. Regardless of the words they use, however, Sevens are generally upbeat, engaging, optimistic, and curious. They focus on possibilities and options, having fun, and keeping others entertained.

When Sevens overdo their Preferred Strategy, "excited" becomes distorted into "irresponsible." Stressed Sevens deal with the world by becoming easily distracted and leaving a trail of unfinished projects in their wake. They may make rash decisions without thinking through the consequences, hoping to charm their way out of the messes they create.

The Neglected Strategy: Striving to be Detached

The strategy at Point Five, Striving to be Detached, in some ways contradicts the Sevens desire to be excited. Detachment, to the Seven, implies being dry, dull, and emotionally flat—the opposite of excitement. Therefore, Sevens become uncomfortable with this strategy and "neglect" it. Rather than seeing the full value of Striving to be appropriately Detached, Sevens distort it and see it as *remoteness*. They may fear that if they are not in the center of activity and fun (if they are *detached*) they will become bored and be seen as boring.

This is not to say that Sevens are incapable of the rigorous intellectual pursuits often seen in Fives. In fact, Sevens have curious minds and are often found in the sciences and academia. However, they tend to be undisciplined with activities they find boring and lose interest quickly in areas that are not highly stimulating.

The Contradiction: Enthusiasm vs. Withholding

The neglect of the natural and healthy desire to detach—to take time for oneself and not feel the need to entertain others—causes Sevens to act out their Neglected Strategy in subtle and predictable ways. Sevens are usually enthusiastic but sometimes they can be withdrawn and emotionally unavailable. For example, they may avoid social settings and interacting with others so they can get relief from their role as group energizer. When Sevens become aware that they are acting this way they will quickly revert to their typical "Seven-ish" behavior of being hyperactive and excitable.

The Support Strategy: Striving to be Perfect

Sevens use Striving to be Perfect to reinforce being excited. They present a socially acceptable persona by being engaging, charming, and likeable in an effort to be thought well of. Sevens generally try to behave in ways that please others: whether by being helpful, socially active, or dutifully filling the role of the entertainer. However, under stress Sevens may become sharply critical of others. They become anxious that others may behave in a way that may hinder the Seven's ability to have fun and get their way. They may present an image that makes others happy but does not reflect the Seven's true thoughts, feelings, or behaviors.

Sevens At Their Best

When Sevens are at their best, they use all three of the strategies naturally and appropriately rather than in the habitual patterns described above. They are enthusiastic and energetic but focused, and they finish what they start; they are able to spend time alone and care for their own needs without being selfish or feeling guilty; and they are rigorous and detail-oriented without being critical and perfectionistic.

Sevens At a Glance

Examples of Sevens: Robin Williams, Steven Spielberg, Bette Midler, Richard Branson, Goldie Hawn, Jim Carrey, Ben Franklin.

Chief Asset: *Enthusiasm.* Sevens have a unique ability to experience enthusiasm for the little things in life. Their happiness and good humor are infectious and inspire those around them to feel good and have fun as well.

What They Like in Others: Optimism, lightheartedness, spontaneity.

What They Dislike in Others: Pessimism, stuffiness, rigidity.

How They Frustrate Others: Hyperactivity, inappropriateness, lack of commitment.

Approach to Problem Solving: "Let's look at the bright side."

Belief About Work: "Things work best when I get to have fun."

How Others See Sevens: Joyful, upbeat, exciting, and energetic, but sometimes irresponsible, distracted, inattentive, and self-centered.

Sevens Get Into Trouble When They Tell Themselves: "Everything will be fine when I get (fill in the blank) or when (fill in the blank) happens."

Blind Spot: *Distractibility.* Sevens are often unaware of their tendency to be easily distracted and its impact on their relationships. Sevens continually attempt to avoid unpleasant thoughts, feelings, and experiences. By not focusing on any one thing for too long, Sevens avoid the possibility of something becoming unpleasant. Because they move from topic to topic so quickly, others may feel ignored or left in the dust.

The Seven Leader: The Enthusiast

The High Side of the Enthusiast: Sevens inspire others with excitement, optimism, and energy and create positive energy toward a shared goal.

The Low Side of the Enthusiast: Sevens can be impractical, easily distracted, impulsive, and irresponsible.

Where They Shine: *At energizing people.* Sevens are great in situations where they have the opportunity to galvanize enthusiasm and energy around a concept, product, cause, etc.

The Enneagram Emotional Competencies

As we have already discussed in Chapter Two, *emotional intelligence* is the ability to (1) identify your emotions and manage your responses to them, and (2) identify the emotions of others and manage your responses to them. The following *emotional competencies* are a set of sixteen specific capabilities based on emotional intelligence. They indicate how well Sevens use emotional intelligence personally and socially.

PERSONAL COMPETENCIES

Self-Awareness

Self-Awareness: ability to identify one's thought processes, emotions, and skills
Typically: Sevens are good at identifying what makes them happy but not always astute at identifying their feelings. They tend to block out any feelings that will make them unhappy, fearful, or uncomfortable. Sevens tend to spend a lot of time thinking about and planning a happy future, and thus they are often out of touch with their present experiences and emotions. They are much better at identifying their skills, but they may overestimate their abilities in the heat and excitement of the moment.
When Stressed: Sevens can jump from one thought to the next in an effort to avoid thoughts and feelings that can lead them to experiencing something unpleasant. While highly identified with the process of thinking, stressed Sevens are simply unaware of what they are currently experiencing because they are so busy thinking about the future. They work hard to avoid seeing their anxieties and the ways in which their own actions have brought about their current troubles and how their behaviors may have had adverse effects on others.

Self-Confidence: confidence in one's powers and abilities
Typically: Sevens are an unusual combination of boldness and insecurity. They may appear to be very confident, even cocky, but inside they may be filled with self-doubt. They are often risk takers and gutsy entrepreneurs, and they trust their ability to think on their feet. The idea of "winging it" provides them with an adrenaline rush that Sevens use to boost their confidence. For Sevens in the planning

stage there is no mountain that cannot be climbed, no idea that is too far-fetched, and no possibility that is too remote.

When Stressed: Sevens may become self-doubting, though this doubt is often masked by bravado. They fear disappointing others, believing that love and benefit may be withheld if they do not measure up to expectations. This fear of failure can cause Sevens to lose confidence and give up a project midstream.

Self-Management

Self-Control: restraint exercised over one's impulses, emotions or desires

Typically: Sevens are the most impulsive of the types, and pride themselves on their spontaneity and their ability to obtain the things that will make them happy. Because they believe that the grass is greener on the other side of the fence, they frequently hop fences. Because ideas are often as energizing to Sevens as actual accomplishments, they may leave tasks unfinished when they are sidetracked by a new whim. Sevens express joy, excitement, and enthusiasm freely and without restraint. In fact, the restraint often seems senseless to Sevens because it takes the fun and excitement out of life.

When Stressed: Sevens struggle even more with self-control. Stress and anxiety make their minds work overtime, and Sevens move into action as a way to stay happy and suppress their anxiety. They fear that if they restrain themselves they will miss out on something that will bring them pleasure or excitement. Stressed Sevens also have a tendency to overindulge in whatever they do, firmly believing that if some is good, more is better.

Adaptability: flexibility in handling change

Typically: Sevens shine in this competency. They seek out and initiate change for the fun and excitement it offers. They see possibilities in creative options and trying new things. Sevens see change as positive, therapeutic, and necessary for the organization and other people, not just for themselves. Sevens are excited by new and attractive ideas and they have a high degree of suggestibility, easily becoming caught up in ideas that are presented to them enthusiastically. They are masterful change agents and excel at initiating new ventures.

When Stressed: Sevens may become easily bored and, if things are going too smoothly, they may make changes just to stir things up.

They may be less patient, and want to move on, break arrangements, commitments, or relationships, regardless of the impact it has on other people. It should be noted, however, that Sevens do not like change being thrust upon them. Such an imposition may heighten their anxiety about the uncertainty of the future and make them feel like their options are limited. Oddly enough, stressed Sevens can also become very rigid in their thoughts and behavior patterns while demanding change from others.

Trustworthiness: *maintaining standards of honesty and integrity*
Typically: If the situation or facts are pleasant, Sevens can maintain high standards of honesty and integrity. They tend to take what is present and try to make it better, as if trying to breathe energy and excitement into day-to-day life. The secret desire of the Seven to withhold and not have to entertain others often leads Sevens to keep secrets about their activities. They present the image of a person who is always "on" and upbeat, when in fact they might prefer to be home relaxing. They prefer to keep this side of themselves hidden from others for fear that it will not be accepted. This hiding may make them appear untrustworthy to others, even though no malice is intended.
When Stressed: Sevens may fall victim to "the little white lie" syndrome. They may stretch the truth, inflate possibilities, put a positive spin on things, and forget to include unpleasant details. As stress increases, they will lie if necessary to avoid being confronted with mistakes they have made, or to avoid the problems they are facing.

Optimism: *ability to anticipate and expect the best possible outcome*
Typically: Sevens are almost off the scale on this competency. They envision a positive future, focus on the great possibilities that the future holds and refuse to let challenges dampen their enthusiasm. Their optimism is contagious and they see possibilities where others do not. Sevens pour so much energy into their vision that they motivate others to align with them and believe in them. Sevens tend to associate with other positive people who will share their enthusiasm and spur them on to even more exciting ideas.
When Stressed: Sevens may work hard to maintain their sense of optimism through reframing—ignoring the objective facts, fantasizing unrealistic outcomes, believing that non-existent resources and people will magically appear to save the day. They begin to rely on others to boost their optimism. Sevens want others to mirror their optimism and become easily disappointed if they do not.

Initiative: readiness to act on opportunities
Typically: This is another high competency for Sevens. They are constantly looking for opportunities and find joy in pursuing them. The impulsiveness of the Seven works to their benefit in this competency. Their spontaneity makes it possible for them to act on opportunities without feeling bound to the current course of action. Sevens find excitement in opportunity and, rather than seeing risk, they see a chance to contribute and have fun. Sevens have a unique ability to get projects started.
When Stressed: Sevens can become indecisive and struggle with taking initiative. They prefer the safety of planning to the danger inherent in doing. They may plan businesses in their heads but may not act on building them. They may plan a vacation to an exotic locale but never leave home. Their impulsiveness can look like initiative, but they may hatch ill-conceived schemes with little hope of being successful. They may spend too much time planning, but plan poorly—incompletely, unrealistically, and dispassionately—often not caring how their acts affect others.

Achievement Drive: striving to meet or improve a standard of excellence
Typically: Sevens enjoy the satisfaction of doing something well—competing and winning are exciting and Sevens thrive on excitement. Sevens are very competitive, usually in a healthy way, and they set challenges for themselves as a way of making life more fun. Upping the ante turns normal activities into "events" and heightens their experience. Sevens often have a drive to make the world a better, more-interesting place, and their optimism makes them feel that they can play a part in doing so.
When Stressed: Sevens expect their achievements to come easily. They may become rigid, critical, and demanding toward people they see as impeding their ability to achieve. If the obstacles to accomplishing their goals become too great, they may begin to doubt their ability and may create a reason for changing course. They may mask their fear of failure by creating a smokescreen of lost interest, distraction, and change of direction.

Resiliency: capacity to endure in the face of obstacles
Typically: Sevens' optimism helps them overcome obstacles. They have the attitude "If life gives you lemons, make lemonade." Their ability to shift focus from the negative to the positive helps them remain resilient. In addition, their quick and agile minds help them

find their way around obstacles—they will find options and possibilities in other places and people.

When Stressed: Sevens sometimes think that projects they take on will be much easier than they estimate. They then become frustrated at roadblocks and may quit prematurely. Their focus on being happy and avoiding pain does not predispose them to dealing well with obstacles when they are under stress. Stressed Sevens may tend to blame others for their misfortune and overlook their own role in creating obstacles. That said, Sevens tend to bounce back from adversity relatively quickly. Once they have caught their breath, they block out the negative and move on.

SOCIAL COMPETENCIES

Attunement to Others

Empathy: awareness of and participation in others' feelings, ideas, and needs
Typically: Sevens are drawn to the joyful feelings, exciting ideas, and needs of others and they are quick to share in someone's joy, excitement, and enthusiasm. They are genuinely happy for the good fortune of others and desire the best for everyone. They are also very aware of a person's less joyful feeling—and boring or tedious ideas and needs—but Sevens may choose not to share in them. In fact, in the same way that Sevens flee from their own negative feelings, they try to avoid being around others who they see as negative. Sevens want those around them to be happy. They may become frustrated with people who are not.

When Stressed: Sevens are focused on keeping their unhappiness at bay by overdoing the things that make them feel better, by making their ideas appear more exciting, and by becoming excessive in meeting their needs. This leaves little room for being aware of or participating in the feelings, ideas, and needs of others.

Political Awareness: reading a group's emotional currents and power relationships
Typically: Sevens generally tune in on the general tenor of a group and classify it either as happy or sad or fun or boring. They often have little patience with analyzing a group on a deeper level. Sevens are better at reading power relationships than at reading emotional currents. They can detect who is in charge, who makes the decisions, and who can meet their needs. Sevens usually have little interest in

power for its own sake—their interest in power and who is wielding power is directly related to how it affects their own well-being. Because they are so personable and fun to be around, Sevens are usually good at aligning themselves with power figures.

When Stressed: Sevens may become self-centered and oblivious to the emotions of others. Stressed Sevens do not want to look at negative emotions, so they may simply ignore the group's negative emotions. They can also become overly sensitive to power issues, fearing that people in power may restrict their freedom.

Communication: listening openly and sending convincing messages
Typically: Sevens are engaging and entertaining conversationalists who love to tell stories and jokes. They are convincing speakers who can build excitement in a group and get team members lined up behind them. Their enthusiasm helps to make them excellent salespersons. However, Sevens generally prefer talking to listening. They often feel that others do not talk fast enough and they have a hard time waiting for their turn to speak. Less-aware Sevens may interrupt often and not allow time for others to interject their ideas.

When Stressed: Sevens have less interest in what others have to say, especially when it is not what they want to hear. If the other's message does not fit their plan, Sevens may reject it and look for something that does. Under stress they prefer their dreams to reality and practice selective listening. Highly stressed Sevens often speak at a dizzying pace, exhibiting their hyperactivity and lack of patience and leaving the listener feeling overwhelmed and exhausted.

Relationship Building

Cooperation: working with others toward shared goals
Typically: Sevens enjoy interacting and working with others. When they are excited about the group's goal, they can be champions of togetherness and stimulate team spirit through sheer enthusiasm. Sevens draw energy from the group and use it to build excitement in themselves, which in turn builds further excitement on the team. They are excellent cheerleaders and take it upon themselves to be the entertainer of the group, the person responsible for seeing that everyone is having a good time.

When Stressed: Sevens may become frustrated with people who do not share their enthusiasm because it makes them feel that they are failing at their role of energizer. Sevens may see cooperation and the idea of working toward shared goals as a threat to the possibility of getting all that they feel they need to be satisfied. As stress mounts, they may fall victim to scarcity thinking and see others as a threat to attaining their share of the limited resources available. They may not purposely undermine others, but they may compete rather than cooperate.

Leadership: *inspiring and leading individuals and groups*

Typically: Sevens' confidence and enthusiasm can inspire groups to find the joy and happiness in themselves and their work. Their optimism fills people with confidence and builds loyalty. People like to work for Sevens because they are fun and exciting to be around them. They create a relaxed environment and use humor and lightheartedness to inspire people. Sevens are usually helpful and caring, making people feel that they are genuinely interested in their welfare and will be there when help is needed. Less-aware Sevens may sometimes use excitement and enthusiasm to cover a lack of a specific, long-term vision.

When Stressed: Sevens start to feel the burden of leadership and become less enthusiastic about the role. Stressed Sevens generally do not like feeling responsible for other people, and their short attention span makes commitment to any long-term goal difficult. Stressed Sevens' willingness to maintain a leadership role diminishes to the degree that they feel hemmed in, bored, or restricted by the demands of leadership.

Influence: *wielding effective tactics for persuasion*

Typically: This is a high competency for Sevens. Sevens are master motivators and often have great skill in swaying others to their point of view. Again, Sevens genuinely want good things to happen for everybody, and they are often charming, engaging and charismatic. Their high energy, optimism, and enthusiasm make them natural salespeople. Sevens are excellent networkers who tend to know a lot of people in a lot of places. They are usually memorable and make an engaging connection with people. This allows them to call in favors, and people are often willing and eager to help them achieve their goals.

When Stressed: Sevens may make false promises and paint rosy pictures to persuade others. It is not that the Seven is being malicious or consciously deceptive; they simply get caught in the energy of the moment and say things that are not thought through. As stress mounts, Sevens can become rigid and demanding. They expect others to change according to their desires but feel they should not have to justify their wants.

Conflict Management: *Negotiating and resolving disputes*

Typically: A self-aware Seven can generally handle open conflict well and usually does so by focusing on the positive. However, Sevens generally try to avoid conflict. Conflict is unpleasant and Sevens work to avoid unpleasant things. If they must resolve a dispute, rather than simply ignore it or delegate it to someone else to handle, they will try to get both sides focused on positive outcomes. They believe that if everyone can focus on an exciting future, problems will solve themselves.

When Stressed: Sevens have a tendency not to address the source of the conflict. They usually retreat first, but they can become combative and demanding that the other person meet their needs regardless of the price the other party has to pay. Stressed Sevens may have a hard time focusing on the other person's side of the story and understanding why others are aggrieved by their behavior.

The Awareness to Action Process

Improving Self-Control

Self-Control is an area where many Sevens struggle. Unlocking the Seven's full capacity for high performance often lies in improving in this competency. What follows is an example of how a Seven might work on this key developmental area; it is not a literal "cook book" for all Sevens, and you may find that improving performance in other competencies is more critical for you. The purpose of this example is to demonstrate how you might use the three steps of The Awareness to Action Process to identify *your* specific developmental areas and improve in those areas.

Other competencies that Sevens would do well to improve in are Trustworthiness and Conflict Management. Self-Control, Trustworthiness, and Conflict Management are interrelated and improvement in one often facilitates improvement in the other two. Trustworthiness means you are accountable and dependable to deliver on your promises; it supports Self-Control by helping you manage the desire to follow your impulses rather than staying focused on commitments. Because Conflict Management involves dealing with disagreements, difficult situations and people, and with unpleasantness in general, skill in Self-Control is extremely helpful in this area.

When formulating your own action plan, work on one or two important goals at a time; create small steps that will move you toward each goal; go from easiest to most difficult, and celebrate your success.

Phase One: Build Awareness

Identify a goal.
- Improve performance in the emotional competency of Self-Control.

Identify your current behaviors.
- "I tend to be impulsive, can become distracted, and may not follow through on important things. I can be insensitive and aggressive in pursuing what I want. Restraint seems senseless to me because it takes the fun and excitement out of life."

Phase Two: Develop Authenticity

Identify how your Preferred Strategy is in conflict with improving in this competency.

- "To me, Striving to be Excited means having fun, staying upbeat, remaining focused on what is pleasant, easy, and satisfying. It involves entertaining others and not holding back in my pursuit of entertainment and my avoidance of what is unpleasant. I feel most comfortable when I don't hold back my enthusiasm and pursuit of pleasure, all of which are in conflict with Self-Control."

Revise your strategy so that it incorporates improvement in this competency. (It should be remembered that when Sevens overdo their Striving to be Excited they may become distracted, fail to meet commitments, make hasty decisions, and act irresponsibly.)

- "Being Excited involves more than the pursuit of immediate pleasure and avoidance of pain. Practicing self-control will help me avoid the irresponsible behaviors that cause me problems now. It will help me focus on long-term happiness rather than short-term pleasure. I can find enjoyment by delving deeply into my experiences rather than skimming across the surface of life in search of the next high point."

Phase Three: Take Action

Devise and Execute an Action Plan; be sure that it involves a goal, action steps, a person who will help monitor your success, and a timeline for completion. See Appendix C for a sample Action Plan. Sample action steps are listed below.

- Practice self-discipline. Notice the impact that overindulgence has on your life, and how often you put yourself first, even when it is not appropriate. Establish limits on what you buy, eat, drink, experience, say, do, etc.
- Be aware of what you do when you begin to experience anxiety or nervousness. Think before you act. Self-control may mean doing nothing in order to avoid doing something inappropriate.
- Stay focused. Be aware of your tendency to label normal, necessary activities as boring, and your tendency to do the fun activities and leave the tedious activities to others.

- Be patient with people. Avoid interrupting, answering and planning for others, and being rude in order to get what you want.
- Do your homework, and don't make decisions based on a whim. Stop to consider the consequences of your behavior.
- See Appendix B, General Recommendations for Growth.

CHAPTER ELEVEN

TYPE EIGHT:
STRIVING TO BE POWERFUL

Power is confident, self-assuring, self-starting and self-stopping, self-warming and self-justifying. When you have it you know it."
RALPH ELLISON

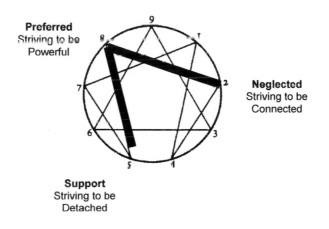

Preferred
Striving to be
Powerful

Neglected
Striving to be
Connected

Support
Striving to be
Detached

Portrait of an Eight

Tom took over McGarvey Printing 20 years ago from his father, who took it over from his father 20 years before that. He has kept the company profitable through good and bad times, sometimes through simple will power and hard work. McGarvey is a small company, employing just over 200 employees, and, as Tom puts it, "we have to kick ass to compete with the big guys." He has never entertained selling the company in his years as its CEO and President. He thrives on a challenge, and is at his best during a crisis.

Tom's boss sees Tom as a natural leader. "He's self-confident and decisive. He likes taking risks and competing with strong adversaries, and he absolutely hates to lose. Tom continues to challenge you until he gets what he wants. He gets the best out of people because he pushes them to do more than even they thought was possible. But his relentlessness can be threatening to some people. For example, when our sales numbers are down Tom is like a dog with a bone—he won't stop driving people until the numbers go back up. The constant pushing can take its toll on people."

McGarvey's plant manager has known Tom for 15 years. "One thing I like about Tom is that he's a straight shooter. You know where you stand with him. If you do your job, he likes you; if you don't, you better figure out how to turn things around or look for another job. He trusts you after a toe-to-toe confrontation. He likes to challenge you, to rant and rave and swear, but that's Tom's style, it's nothing personal."

His administrative assistant told us that Tom has done things for employees that most people don't know about, like giving a shipping clerk a $5,000 interest-free loan to help pay the medical expenses for his sick child. "He's seen as a tough boss, and he encourages people to see him that way, but Tom takes care of his people."

Some of his employees only see one side of Tom, and are unimpressed by his "Champion of the People" persona. One of his managers told us, "He has to dominate every meeting, every conversation. I had what I thought was a great idea about improving quality that Tom didn't agree with. I discussed my point with solid facts and he attacked the idea with even more energy. When I argued back, he exploded and attacked me personally, saying I was 'stupid.' He apologized to me later, but the damage had been done."

When asked to identify himself, Tom said he was self-confident, in control, organized, assertive, direct, honest, judgmental, generous, decisive, and a problem solver. "I know that sounds cold and analytical to some people, but that's me. The part of me that I seldom talk about is the guarded side—my more emotional, sensitive side; the part that I seldom express, especially in public. I'm very uncomfortable feeling out of control or showing any vulnerability."

Tom is an Eight. Of course, not all Eights have exactly the same traits that Tom does, but some of his characteristics will resonate with you if you are an Eight. You may also recognize some of these behaviors if you know an Eight. Tom, like all Eights, is motivated by striving to be powerful.

The rest of this chapter explores the personality dynamics of Eights and shows how they can improve performance in the emotional competencies.

The Strategies

The Preferred Strategy: Striving to be Powerful

Eights interact with the world by Striving to be Powerful. Different Eights may use different words for "Striving to be Powerful," such as wanting to be strong, independent, in control, assertive, etc. Regardless of the words they use, however, Eights are action-oriented self-starters who love to be in charge. They focus on getting things done and overcoming any obstacles that may lie in their way.

When Eights overdo their Preferred Strategy, "powerful" becomes distorted into "uncontrolled." Stressed Eights deal with the world by being aggressive, forceful, domineering, and angry. They may not adhere to the rules or norms that others expect them to follow and their behavior can become impulsive and rash.

The Neglected Strategy: Striving to be Connected

The strategy at Point Two, "Striving to be Connected," in some ways contradicts the Eight's Striving to be Powerful. After all, connecting to others makes it difficult to be autonomous, and connecting to their feelings makes it difficult for Eights to be strong and invulnerable. Therefore, Eights are uncomfortable with this strategy and "neglect" it. Rather than see the full value of being connected, Eights distort it and see it as *dependence*. They fear that if they reach out to others they will be seen as weak.

This is not to say that Eights are incapable of emotion or having close relationships. In fact, Eights are often very warm and have deep and lasting relationships. However, their emotional displays are usually from a place of magnanimity and strength rather than vulnerability (such as showing deep compassion for the down-trodden, but not for those struggling with the normal trials of daily life). While passionate and protective, they are usually very private about their feelings for the people close to them.

The Contradiction: Assertiveness vs. Neediness

The neglect or repression of the natural and healthy desire for connection causes Eights to act out the Neglected Strategy in subtle and predictable ways. Eights are usually assertive, but sometimes may become needy. For example, they may demand emotional support and appreciation from the people close to them. When Eights become aware that they are behaving this way they will quickly revert to their typical "Eight-ish" behavior of being autonomous and stoic.

The Support Strategy: Striving to be Detached

Eights use Striving to be Detached to reinforce their Striving to be Powerful. They are shrewd strategic thinkers who can step back from a situation, analyze it clearly, and make difficult decisions. They can ignore fatigue, setbacks, and obstacles in pursuit of their goals. However, under stress Eights can become withdrawn, moody, and insensitive to other people's needs. They may withhold information as a way to manipulate and control others.

Eights At Their Best

When Eights are at their best they use all three of the strategies naturally and appropriately rather than habitually. They are powerful and decisive without being domineering; they are comfortably connected to others without feeling that they must be in control of the relationship; and they are objective without being cold and remote.

Eights At a Glance

Examples of Eights: John Wayne, Donald Trump, Charlton Heston, Ann Coulter, Roseanne Barr, Sean Penn, Susan Sarandon.

Chief Asset: *Passion.* Eights are robust and energetic. They bring great passion and determination to whatever they undertake.

What They Like in Others: Confidence, lack of pretense, straightforwardness.

What They Dislike in Others: Timidity, bullying, rigidity.

How They Frustrate Others: Arrogance, hostility, stubbornness.

Approach to Problem Solving: "It's time for me to take charge."

Belief About Work: "Things work best when I'm in control."

How Others See Eights: Honest, outgoing, fun-loving, and strong-willed, but sometimes blunt, excessive, reckless, and arrogant.

Eights Get Into Trouble When They Tell Themselves: "The world is a threatening place that will not cut me a break. I must take from life anything good that I can get."

Blind Spot: *Abusiveness.* Eights are often unaware of their tendency to be abusive and its affect on their relationships. They don't see that others view their "straight talk and tough love" as abuse. Although they claim that they are trying to help by being honest and fair, they are often lashing out at the weakness and incompetence they see in others and fear seeing in themselves.

The Eight Leader: The Commander

The High Side of the Commander: Eights are decisive, bold, and confident, and inspire these qualities in their followers.

The Low Side of the Commander: Eights can be arrogant, hostile, and demanding, and may focus on their own agenda rather than the good of the group

Where They Shine: *When the going gets tough.* Eights bring tremendous self-confidence and energy to their work, and they thrive in the heat of battle. They love a challenge to overcome.

The Enneagram Emotional Competencies

As we have already discussed in Chapter Two, *emotional intelligence* is the ability to (1) identify your emotions and manage your responses to them, and (2) identify the emotions of others and manage your responses to them. The following *emotional competencies* are a set of sixteen specific capabilities based on emotional intelligence. They indicate how well Eights use emotional intelligence personally and socially.

PERSONAL COMPETENCIES

Self-Awareness

Self-Awareness: ability to identify one's thought processes, emotions, and skills
Typically: Eights are good at identifying their skills, fair at identifying their thought processes, but not very good at identifying their emotional states. They tend to see things in black and white; they know what they like and dislike and are vocal about what pleases and displeases them. Eights tend to avoid introspection and looking too deeply for ambiguities. They are also not very astute at identifying the emotional impact they have on others.
When Stressed: Eights lose touch with their thought processes and begin to act before considering the possible results of their actions. Their thinking becomes cloudy. They may demonize people, become paranoid, and often find themselves acting too hastily and later regretting their behavior. They may overestimate their skills and have an inflated view of their importance.

Self-Confidence: confidence in one's powers and abilities
Typically: Eights are very high in self-confidence. Their approach to interacting with the world is to seek to gain power in whatever way they can, and Eights seem to innately have the confidence necessary to gain power. They have spent their whole lives testing themselves and searching for challenges. By taking on increasingly greater challenges—and meeting them—they get a feel for both what they are good at and what they are not good at. Through this feedback process they gain even more self-confidence.
When Stressed: Eights can become defensive, and much of their apparent self-confidence may be merely bluster that hides a perceived vulnerability. They have difficulty accepting failure, and the thought

of not being in control of a challenging situation can make them even more aggressive.

Self-Management

Self-Control: restraint exercised over one's impulses, emotions or desires

Typically: Eights do not exercise great impulse control. They rarely see the value in holding back or exercising caution. The longer they wait to take action, the more uncomfortable and vulnerable they feel, so they tend to follow their first impulse. Regarding desires, *they want what they want when they want it* and do not see why they should not have it. They repress their fear and anxiety, and control any behavior that would appear to leave them vulnerable. Even though they may be experiencing aggression internally, self-aware Eights have learned not to act it out.

When Stressed: Eights respond immediately and explosively to stimuli. This area gets Eights into the most trouble in organizational situations and environments. They may have trouble controlling their anger even if it involves hurting other people's feelings. Stressed Eights often see restraint as weakness, indecisiveness, or procrastination. "Don't just sit there, do something," is one of their mottos. They may glory in their impulsiveness, see it as a strength, and will do whatever it takes to fulfill their desires.

Adaptability: flexibility in handling change

Typically: Eights do not respond well to change that is forced upon them but are good at creating change. Because they feel such a strong need to be in control, when change is imposed on them, strong emotions, such as anger and betrayal, may be triggered. Initiating change, however, strengthens their sense of control. They can be effective agents of change, and their passion can energize and mobilize people to embrace new ideas and action plans.

When Stressed: Eights become combative when change is imposed on them. They may become disruptive, resistant, and will likely try to undermine those imposing the change. They will defend their own ideas, not wanting to give ground. They may issue ultimatums and become stubborn and aggressive.

Trustworthiness: maintaining standards of honesty and integrity

Typically: Eights value integrity, fairness, and justice, so they try hard to be fair and honest models of integrity. Because they have high expectations of others in this area, they often hold themselves to high standards as well. Eights are straight shooters—they rarely sugarcoat their opinions. In fact, they often verbalize exactly what they are thinking, regardless of whether it hurts other people's feelings, and with little regard for the consequences of their statements.

When Stressed: When Eights feel they are being treated unfairly, the gloves come off, and they will do what it takes to come out on top, even if it means being deceitful and fighting unfairly. They rationalize their aggressive behavior and feel that the other person does not deserve to be treated fairly and with integrity. Highly stressed Eights focus on their desires and needs and can be guided, not by integrity, but by simple self-interest.

Optimism: ability to anticipate and expect the best possible outcome
Typically: Eights are optimistic when they feel they have a sense of control in a given matter; they believe that things will go well if they are at the helm. Their optimism and belief in themselves can be infectious. However, if they sense that others are in control or have more influence than they should, Eights are not optimistic that things will work out for the best. They will be more vigilant, reactive, and questioning of those in command, often looking for roadblocks to other people's plans.

When Stressed: Eights tend to become pessimistic and, in their paranoia, seek out possibilities of danger and failure. They see the worst in people and situations, and they tend to see potential trouble in harmless people and places. Their negativity may be the cause of failure of a project or initiative. Also, their aggressive behavior often leads to self-fulfilling prophecy.

Initiative: readiness to act on opportunities
Typically: Eights want to make things happen and look for a chance to show what they are made of. Because of their high energy they find it difficult not to show initiative. Because their attention is focused outward, Eights are constantly looking for opportunities to exert their will and to use their strength and energy. Eights try to make a positive change when possible and to have an impact on their environment.

When Stressed: Eights often use their initiative against those they see as enemies. They become proactively combative and pick fights with those they see as potential threats. An enemy can focus their attention, and a cause can help them mount an all-out campaign to dominate an opponent. "Taking the initiative" can translate into "fight to win" or "take no prisoners," depending on how stressed the Eight may be.

Achievement Drive: striving to meet or improve a standard of excellence
Typically: Eights see standards as challenges and opportunities to test themselves. Exceeding standards, breaking records, and being the best energizes them. They are highly competitive and will often not settle for established standards but will instead want to test themselves against increasingly higher standards.
When Stressed: Eights use achievement drive as a way to establish their dominance and to be seen as the boss (the "Alpha male" syndrome). They may push themselves and others harder and harder, to see "what you're made of" and to test themselves against others.

Resiliency: capacity to endure in the face of obstacles
Typically: Eights take pride in their capacity to endure suffering, to "take a good punch," and overcome obstacles. They subscribe wholeheartedly to the expression, "When the going gets tough, the tough get going." They love to have their will tested because it reassures them of their sense of being powerful and in control. Eights can also be stoic in the face of hardship and can take pride in enduring more than anyone else in order to test their mettle.
When Stressed: Eights may start to complain, and perhaps even exaggerate the hardships they are facing, but they use this as a way to energize themselves. The more fast and furious the obstacles arise, the more aggressive Eights become, reacting strongly, even brutally, to defeat the competition. Highly stressed Eights tend to overreact in the face of obstacles and may use much more force and energy than is needed.

SOCIAL COMPETENCIES

Attunement to Others

Empathy: awareness of and participation in others' feelings, ideas, and needs
Typically: Some Eights may have developed the capacity to be aware of and feel what others are feeling, but this is not a skill that comes easily to them. Eights sometimes seem to be unconscious of the feelings and needs of others. Because Eights can be stoic and can disregard their own emotions and needs, they have a tendency to

overlook those of others as well. Further, because they feel that each person should stand up for his or her own needs, Eights do not feel a need to do it for them.

When Stressed: Eights may feel contempt toward themselves for having needs and emotions because they see them as weaknesses. Stressed Eights project this contempt onto others when they see their feelings and needs. They may belittle people who show their feelings and may ridicule or punish them for "being weak."

Political Awareness: reading a group's emotional currents and power relationships

Typically: Eights are good at reading power relationships but not as good at reading emotional currents. They intuitively understand where the power lies in a group. They know how to gain and wield power, but they may fall short when it comes to taking others' emotions into consideration when applying power. They often lack the ability to discriminate finer distinctions in emotions and may therefore miss subtle emotional signals from others.

When Stressed: Eights may see dissent and group dissatisfaction where it may not exist and tend to project their own disappointment onto others, thereby misreading the tone of the group. For example, they may see the group's normal degree of anxiety before a product launch as weakness and lack of trust. Highly stressed Eights often perceive authority figures as unjust and peers as competitors in the struggle for power.

Communication: listening openly and sending convincing messages

Typically: Eights are better at sending convincing messages than at listening to others. Eights firmly believe that they already know the truth, so they may sometimes fail to listen fully to others. They can become impatient and may interrupt others in an effort to state their own opinions. Eights advance their ideas with passion and power, and are influential communicators. They can mobilize people to believe in their agendas, and they can use their enthusiasm and belief in themselves to gain the trust of others. Unfortunately, other people's messages often get lost in the wake of Eights' passionate expression of their ideas.

When Stressed: Eights can become bullying, loud, demanding, and abusive. They may issue orders rather than engage in dialogue. Often they do not tolerate disagreement but may steadfastly resist hearing other points of view, believing that their ideas are the only ones with any value.

Relationship Building

Cooperation: working with others toward shared goals

Typically: "Cooperation" to Eights often means that others are cooperating with them, not that they are cooperating with others. They usually take it upon themselves to establish goals for the whole group and then convince others to embrace *those* goals. However, self-aware Eights can work toward shared goals, but they have a difficult time not seeing themselves as the leader. They are able to cooperate in limited partnerships and smaller groups more easily than in larger groups.

When Stressed: Eights do not easily share goals that are established by others. In fact, they often take pleasure in challenging group goals and changing them when it may not be necessary. Eights become uncooperative and refuse to bow to the pressure of the group. They espouse the belief "It's my way or the highway," and may sabotage the objectives and efforts of others in order to gain control.

Leadership: inspiring and leading individuals and groups

Typically: Eights are natural leaders who seek and feel comfortable in leadership roles. Others feel comfortable with Eights as leaders because they are protective, fair, and honest. They take a personal interest in the welfare of those they lead and are capable of showing great compassion and generosity to those whom they have taken under their wing. Eights make decisions more quickly and confidently than any other type, so others naturally find themselves willingly following their lead.

When Stressed: Eights may use their leadership skills to manipulate others and meet their own needs. Stressed Eights tend to lead by intimidating, overpowering, and browbeating people into submission. Their agendas may be self-serving, but stressed Eights can sometimes still manage to get others to follow them or do their bidding by sheer power of will.

Influence: wielding effective tactics for persuasion

Typically: Eights use their passion and intensity to sway others to their way of thinking. Self-aware Eights direct this ability toward the good of the group. Eights combine their self-confidence and leadership ability to create excitement in others. They are direct and convincing and leave no doubt about where they stand. They are excellent strategic and tactical thinkers and innately know how to influence others to get things done.

When Stressed: Eights can be manipulative and Machiavellian, and they use their gifts of influence to advance their own cause and do harm to their real or perceived enemies. Eights may overdo their efforts to influence others and may use highly aggressive means to get their point across. Highly stressed Eights manipulate through personal power, money, and other means of coercion.

Conflict Management: Negotiating and resolving disputes
Typically: Eights have a tendency to enjoy some degree of conflict. Having a cause to fight for or an opponent to battle energizes them and makes life more interesting. During conflict, they state their agenda well but do not listen to others very well. They see their desires as more important than the desires of others and tend to make demands rather than requests. They often move to action too quickly, failing to consider others' feelings or perspectives. They are great to have around when an organization is facing difficult times, but when times are calm they may get bored and look for battles to fight just to liven things up.
When Stressed: Eights are easily drawn into conflict. They believe that life is a battlefield and that potential enemies are everywhere. Because they have a tendency to demonize their opponent, they are not very good at resolving disputes and may not have any desire to make peace. They try to resolve conflict by force rather than negotiation and are only satisfied when the other side concedes.

The Awareness to Action Process

Improving Empathy

Empathy is an area where many Eights struggle. Unlocking the Eight's full capacity for high performance often lies in improving in this competency. What follows is an example of how an Eight might work on this key developmental area; it is not a literal "cook book" for all Eights, and you may find that improving performance in other competencies is more critical for you. The purpose of this example is to demonstrate how you might use the three steps of The Awareness to Action Process to identify *your* specific developmental areas and improve in those areas.

Other competencies that Eights would do well to improve in are Self-Control and Communication. Empathy, Self-Control, and Communication are interrelated and improvement in one often facilitates improvement in the other two. Empathy is the awareness of and participation in others' feelings, ideas, and needs; it also involves communicating with sensitivity and openness. Self-control involves restraint over one's impulses, emotions or desires, as well as controlling impatience and aggressiveness. Skill in both self-control and communication are essential to improvement in empathy.

When formulating your own action plan, work on one or two important goals at a time; create small steps that will move you toward each goal; go from easiest to most difficult, and celebrate your success.

Phase One: Build Awareness

Identify a goal.
- Improve performance in the emotional competency of Empathy.

Identify your current behaviors.
- "I expect others to be as tough as I am. I push people very hard and when they complain I can become cutting and sarcastic. Rather than recognizing their feelings, I can be impatient and often I don't listen well; I don't notice how my forcefulness often overwhelms others."

Phase Two: Develop Authenticity

Identify how your Preferred Strategy is in conflict with improving in this competency.

- "To me, Striving to be Powerful means expressing my will, and letting people see that I am strong and in charge. I believe 'tough love' is a more-effective way to treat people than coddling them. Being empathetic can leave me vulnerable. If people see me as soft they will take advantage of me and I won't be as effective in getting things done."

Revise your strategy so that it incorporates improvement in this competency. (Remember that when Eights overdo their Striving to be Powerful their behavior can become uncontrolled).

- "Real power is the ability to express my will and to get things done. The more I can get people to work with me, the more powerful I am. By showing kindness, sensitivity, and empathy I can create relationships with people who will be loyal to me and help me accomplish my vision."

Phase Three: Take Action

Devise and Execute an Action Plan; be sure that it involves a goal, action steps, a person who will help monitor your success, and a timeline for completion. See Appendix C for a sample Action Plan. Sample action steps are listed below.

- Accept the fact that others have no desire to be as "tough" as you. Don't judge people negatively for their sensitivity. Work at understanding that sensitivity is just as valuable as toughness.
- Practice simple kindness and politeness: be patient; say "Good morning," "Please," and "Thank you."
- Learn to say, "I'm sorry," whenever appropriate. Apologizing, and recognizing when you need to apologize, is the most powerful step in developing empathy.
- Before ending conversations, politely ask others if they have anything to say before you move on.
- Ask a coworker to tell you when you are inattentive, abrupt, bossy, interrupting, or dominating the conversation.
- See Appendix B, General Recommendations for Growth.

CHAPTER TWELVE

TYPE NINE:
STRIVING TO BE PEACEFUL

*Peace is not the absence of war; it is a virtue, a state of mind, a
disposition of benevolence, confidence and justice.*
BARUCH SPINOZA

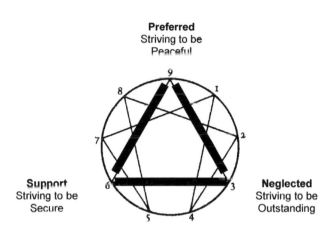

Preferred
Striving to be
Peaceful

Support
Striving to be
Secure

Neglected
Striving to be
Outstanding

Portrait of a Nine

Deborah is the director of Art and Design for a national toy
manufacturer. She manages a staff of six designers and an
administrative assistant, and she oversees an annual budget of three
million dollars. Part of her job is to interact with the marketing,
finance, and product-development departments. "I wouldn't want her
job," her boss told us. "She's the final decision maker for every
design, every piece of art, and every word that appears on our
products. She also has to coordinate efforts between a variety of
departments within the company, and with outside vendors. Quite
often the needs of these groups are very different from one another."

Deborah is a natural mediator. She can empathize with both
marketing's needs to reach more customers in the Pacific Northwest
and finance's need to meet budget constraints. At product launch
meetings, she gets people to think like a team. As the director of
marketing puts it, "She has an effortless way of bringing all of us
together. She listens to each person's point of view and articulates it
back to the team in a way that blends it into a common goal. She

helps us see the overall objective and the broader view—she calls it 'the view from 30,000 feet'—so that it's not so difficult to come to a consensus as a group."

However, some people who work with Deborah feel that she has little sense of urgency, isn't aggressive enough, and avoids making decisions out of fear of offending someone. Others will tell you that she's stubborn and not as nice as she appears to be. "Deborah can be a charmer, and while she doesn't always show her anger, she can be argumentative and resistant to other points of view when she becomes frustrated," said one coworker. "When she feels put upon by others she becomes remote and unresponsive."

"She's basically a 'hands-off' manager," said a senior designer. "She gives broad directives, delegates authority and responsibility, and lets you run with a project. That works fine if you're independent and experienced, but some people need more input and direction from her."

Deborah is sometimes amazed that she is in a director level position because she insists that being in charge has never been a need or a goal for her. "I don't see myself as highly competitive," she told us. "I like to play tennis, but I'd rather keep the ball in play than play for points. I run five miles three times a week but I've never been in a race, nor have I ever had the desire to run a marathon. I'd describe myself as pleasant, easy-going, patient, and trusting. I can also be hard-nosed and disagreeable if I feel like I'm being ignored. I just don't express my anger very aggressively."

Deborah is a Nine. Of course, not all Nines have exactly the same traits that Deborah does, but some of her characteristics will resonate with you if you are a Nine. You may also recognize some of these behaviors if you know a Nine. Deborah, like all Nines, is motivated by striving to be peaceful.

The rest of this chapter explores the personality dynamics of Nines and shows how they can improve performance in the emotional competencies.

The Strategies

The Preferred Strategy: Striving to be Peaceful

Nines interact with the world by Striving to be Peaceful. Different Nines may use different words for "Striving to be Peaceful," such as wanting to be composed, relaxed, nice, non-confrontational, self-deprecating, etc. Regardless of the words they use, however, Nines are calm, pleasant, and friendly. They focus on maintaining a sense of inner harmony by minimizing their own needs while concentrating on the needs of others.

When Nines overdo their Preferred Strategy, "peacefulness" becomes distorted into "passivity." Stressed Nines will deal with the world by avoiding the people, events, or tasks that disturb their inner calm. They may resist making decisions and taking action, and they may naively overlook threats to their well-being, security, or success.

The Neglected Strategy: Striving to be Outstanding

The strategy at Point Three, Striving to be Outstanding, in some ways contradicts the Nine's desire to be peaceful. After all, standing out and being in the spotlight can cause the very disruption to their calm that Nines wish to avoid. Therefore, Nines are uncomfortable with this strategy and "neglect" it. Rather than see the full value of being outstanding, Nines distort it and see it as *attention-seeking*. They fear that if they place too much importance on themselves and bring attention to their needs they will be seen as arrogant and demanding. Such behavior would reduce their ability to remain peacefully connected to others.

This is not to say that Nines are incapable of being outstanding and highly accomplished. In fact, Nines are as successful in life as any other type. However, their accomplishment is often accompanied by self-deprecation and Nines often seem to be uncomfortable with attention being brought to their successes.

The Contradiction: Self-Sacrificing vs. Self-Centered

The neglect or repression of the natural and healthy desire for attention causes Nines to act out the Neglected Strategy in subtle and predictable ways. Nines are usually self-sacrificing, but sometimes they become self-centered. For example, though they often ignore their own needs and desires, at times they become frustrated at sacrificing for everyone else and selfishly focus on their own wants. When Nines become aware that they are behaving this way they will quickly revert to their typical "Nine-ish" behavior of being self-deprecating and unassuming.

The Support Strategy: Striving to be Secure

Nines use Striving to be Secure to reinforce their Striving to be Peaceful. They seek safety in familiar and habitual routines and try to maintain the status quo. They are also conscious of what might hurt or offend others and they try to shelter people from harm. Under stress, Nines may become too conservative and averse to taking chances or making changes; they may studiously ignore situations or events that will disturb their inner calm, an approach that can lead to greater problems in the long run.

Nines At Their Best

When Nines are at their best, they use all three of the strategies naturally and appropriately rather than habitually. They are peaceful but decisive and proactive; they are comfortable with acknowledging their own needs as well as their accomplishments; and they are willing to take risks and act on opportunities that take them out of their comfort zone.

Nines at a Glance

Examples of Nines: Ronald Reagan, Laura Bush, Dwight D. Eisenhower, Adam Sandler, Willie Nelson, Ray Romano, Abraham Lincoln.

Chief Asset: *Balance.* Nines have a capacity to remain immovable, solid, and unfazed by the turmoil around them. They can make people feel safe and have a calming, anxiety-reducing effect on others.

What They Like in Others: Optimism, humility, consistency.

What They Dislike in Others: Confrontation, arrogance, turbulence.

How They Frustrate Others: Passive-aggression, withdrawing, indecision.

Approach to Problem Solving: "Let's get together and hear what everyone has to say."

Belief About Work: "Things work best when there is harmony and nobody makes waves."

How Others See Nines: Pleasant, likable, levelheaded, and easygoing, but sometimes unfocused, stubborn, and forgetful.

Nines Get Into Trouble When They Tell Themselves: "Other people's needs are more important than my own and I should just go with the flow."

Blind Spot: *Passive-Aggressiveness.* Nines are often unaware of their tendency to get their way passively rather than actively and the impact this has on their relationships. For instance, they may get out of performing an unpleasant task by dragging their feet, being forgetful, making promises that they do not keep, and so forth. Others are often frustrated by their seeming stubbornness.

The Nine Leader: The Consensus Builder

The High Side of the Consensus Builder: Nines gain commitment through inclusion and participation and make others feel valued by seeking their perspective.

The Low Side of the Consensus Builder: Nines can be indecisive and conflict averse, and may seem to lack their own opinions and vision.

Where They Shine: Helping people feel good about themselves. Nines are great at making people feel included and part of a team. Their calm rubs off on others and helps them relax.

The Enneagram Emotional Competencies

As we have already discussed in Chapter Two, *emotional intelligence* is the ability to (1) identify your emotions and manage your responses to them, and (2) identify the emotions of others and manage your responses to them. The following *emotional competencies* are a set of sixteen specific capabilities based on emotional intelligence. They indicate how well Nines use emotional intelligence personally and socially.

PERSONAL COMPETENCIES

Self-Awareness

Self-Awareness: ability to identify one's thought processes, emotions, and skills
Typically: Nines are more interested in focusing on others than they are in focusing on themselves. They may see their own good qualities, but they often are quick to point out their own flaws. Their need to feel and appear composed makes them reluctant to look deeply at their negative thoughts and emotions. In particular, Nines are often unaware of their anger. They see it as a particularly negative emotion, and they work hard to repress it.
When Stressed: Nines tend to undervalue their skills and abilities. They may not be aware of their positive impact on others, how well they accomplish a project, the depth of their knowledge, etc. They begin to function as if on autopilot, moving through life while trying not to be affected by it. Nines feel that life is something happening around and to them, rather than something that they are participating in.

Self-Confidence: confidence in one's powers and abilities
Typically: While many Nines are successful and industrious, this is generally not a strong area for Nines. Nines are often self-deprecating and have a tendency not to trust their own power and ability to take instinctive action. They avoid the discomfort of their self-perceived shortcomings by aligning with more powerful and confident people, willingly taking on a support role. Some Nines are underachievers because they have difficulty recognizing and using their own powers and abilities in practical ways. More-aware Nines are confident of their ability to work with people, gain trust, and get things done.

When Stressed: Nines can feel their lack of confidence acutely and become hesitant to act. The demands of showing their skills and abilities so drains the stressed Nine's energy that they go along with the crowd or become resigned to following the path of least resistance.

Self-Management

Self-Control: restraint exercised over one's impulses, emotions, or desires
Typically: Nines are controlled in a natural, effortless way. They are generally conscientious and composed, believing that making waves is counterproductive and will cause them and others unnecessary conflict. They desire to build a stable environment, one that is steady, predictable, and comfortable—a workplace where people get along and work effectively together. They follow policies and procedures and go about their work unpretentiously. Nines exercise restraint in pursuing their own desires and impulses and believe that others should also exercise restraint for the good of the group.
When Stressed: Nines give in to their natural impulse towards inertia. They lose themselves in daydreams, books, television, "hanging out," and the like. They succumb to wasting time with nonessential activities, rather than doing essential work. Under increased stress, they may no longer contain their suppressed anger, and inappropriate and misdirected behavior can occur. They can be stubborn, passive aggressive, shut down, and depressed.

Adaptability: flexibility in handling change
Typically: Nines may have difficulty handling change that pulls them out of their comfort zones. Seeking to maintain a steady and comfortable environment, they are on guard against anything that will disrupt it. They find many ways to resist change, but they usually do so passively—dragging their feet, agreeing outwardly while resisting inwardly, becoming forgetful about new procedures, etc. However, once the change occurs, Nines are able to adapt and thrive. They may need to be dragged to the party, but once they get there they have a great time.
When Stressed: Nines resist more strenuously. Having to make the effort to learn something new, such as a new computer program or a new policy, can be difficult for a stressed Nine. They can become stubborn and argumentative, often simply refusing to make changes.

Trustworthiness: maintaining standards of honesty and integrity
Typically: Nines score high in this area. Lying to others or acting without integrity would make it difficult for Nines to maintain their internal sense of well-being. They are also very trusting of others, choosing to see the best in people. Nines find it easy to connect with others and find it difficult to hurt and deceive people. They expect the same from others and are often surprised when the people they are dealing with lack integrity.
When Stressed: Nines become passively deceitful and may lie through omission rather than commission. They agree to things outwardly, but their actions—and often their inaction—serve to undermine agreements. In an effort to fit in and feel liked, they may agree to do certain things and take on roles that in their heart they do not agree with.

Optimism: ability to anticipate and expect the best possible outcome
Typically: Nines tend to see the best in other people; they have an innate trust that everything will work out fine and that the world is a safe place. In general they trust that people will get along, treat each other fairly, and work toward mutual benefit. A focus on positive thinking helps them maintain their sense of inner tranquility. Even when unexpected obstacles come along, Nines often put a positive spin on them as lessons to be learned. Sometimes Nines can be overly optimistic, becoming unrealistic and not seeing trouble on the horizon.
When Stressed: Nines can become indifferent and lose their optimism without becoming particularly pessimistic. They can lose interest in the highs and lows of either optimism or pessimism and settle into a gray middle area that has noncommittal and flat qualities. Under significant stress they may become fatalistic, depressed, and focus on worst-case scenarios, and at times become paralyzed by anxiety.

Initiative: readiness to act on opportunities
Typically: Nines can struggle with beginning projects and initiating action. They work to maintain the status quo and find comfort in the stability of the tried and true. This is not to imply that Nines are not industrious; they can be extremely productive and hard working. Once they overcome their initial inertia, they gain great energy and achieve what they set their minds to. Their efforts, however, are often intended to make others happy rather than making themselves happy.
When Stressed: Nines' lack of confidence often makes them feel that they are lacking something critical—training, education, practice,

etc.—and they become hesitant to act. They tend to focus on the difficulties inherent in an opportunity, finding reasons to avoid acting on it. They have a tendency to rehearse for life rather than live it, and they procrastinate and scatter their energy by doing unimportant tasks to avoid the risks involved in a new endeavor.

Achievement Drive: *striving to meet or improve a standard of excellence*
Typically: Nines have a secret desire to be seen as successful but feel that if their success is too visible they may be perceived as boastful and lose the positive regard of others. Nines adopt a style of effortless achievement and almost seem surprised when others notice their accomplishments. They are creative and find ways to improve on how things are done while still staying within a comfortable range. Their improvements tend to be incremental rather than revolutionary.
When Stressed: Nines can lack confidence that they have the drive, energy or stamina to achieve great things. They may even struggle to simply meet standards, let alone improve upon or exceed them. Highly stressed Nines' natural self-effacement can become overwhelming, and they question why others would value their contributions

Resiliency: *capacity to endure in the face of obstacles*
Typically: The positive outlook and patience of Nines helps them endure in the face of obstacles. They have a fundamental belief that things will work out for the best in the long run. At their best, Nines are adept at going with the flow, focusing on the positive and accepting obstacles as a normal part of life. Their ability to look at the big picture puts obstacles in perspective, and Nines are often able to convey this sense of perspective and optimism to others.
When Stressed: Nines believe that life should be easy and smooth running. Under stress, they may ignore obstacles, refusing to see or feel their impact. Stressed Nines hunker down and wait for things to blow over. Nines may begin to lose perspective and find obstacles to be threatening and overwhelming. They may become anxious and make mountains out of molehills, vacillating between anger and anxiety. Highly stressed Nines may feel trapped and believe that their efforts to change their situation are fruitless.

SOCIAL COMPETENCIES

Attunement to Others

Empathy: awareness of and participation in others' feelings, ideas, and needs
Typically: Nines easily identify with other people—not only with their agendas, but also with their needs, discomforts, and hurts. Nines genuinely care about others' welfare and are interested in their feelings and ideas. Because Nines have a tendency to identify with others and seek common ground, they are often on the lookout for a way to connect. They do this naturally and are energized by the lives and interests of others.
When Stressed: Nines have a tendency to ignore or block out anything that disturbs their inner calm. They will often react with frustration or anger when forced to face the unpleasantness of someone else's negative emotions, needs, or ideas with which they disagree.

Political Awareness: reading a group's emotional currents and power relationships
Typically: Nines usually have a high degree of political awareness. They focus on others and can easily perceive other people's perspectives and positions. Nines tend to excel more at reading emotional currents than at reading power relationships. They are particularly aware in matters of inclusiveness—they can focus on who is being excluded, who is not being heard, who is not being valued, etc. Because they are generally trusting, they are sometimes naïve and often overlook the self-interest, manipulations, and dishonesty of others.
When Stressed: Nines become disinterested in the conflict inherent in office politics and resist becoming involved. Rather than expend the energy required to assess currents, they withdraw. Nines have a tendency, however, to reach a boiling point in this area. They will only remain disengaged for so long before their frustration wells up and inspires them to re-engage.

Communication: listening openly and sending convincing messages
Typically: Nines are usually great listeners. They are generally interested in the views of others. Because they are pleasant, inclusive, and easy-going, Nines tend to be convincing communicators, instilling a sense of trust and comfort in the listener. Sometimes,

however, they may be giving the impression that they are interested while in fact they are daydreaming, caught up in their own thoughts, or listening to other conversations.

When Stressed: Their communication style often becomes a lack of communication, or at least a lack of clear communication. Nines do not want to hear or deliver any news that will disturb the sense of inner calm that they are struggling to hold on to. Nines may try to protect the group—and themselves—from bad news by sugarcoating, procrastinating, or simply neglecting to deliver it. Disconnection and a lack of precision may characterize their conversation style. Paradoxically, as stress increases, they may become argumentative, trying to get others to agree with them in an effort to re-establish inner calm.

Relationship Building

Cooperation: working with others toward shared goals
Typically: Nines see cooperation as an essential virtue, and pride themselves on their ability to get along with others and work as part of a team. They work hard to align their goals with the goals of the group and they become energized by a common vision. Nines generally value collaboration, or at least the appearance of collaboration, over competition.

When Stressed: Nines vacillate between wanting to be left alone and wanting to be part of the group. They often want to do both at the same time and thus swing from willingly working with others to becoming resigned and just going along half-heartedly. In an effort to appear likable and cooperative, they may agree to things that go against their own better judgment. As stress increases, Nines may withdraw and become passive-aggressive and stubborn, believing that not objecting is the same as cooperating.

Leadership: inspiring and leading individuals and groups
Typically: Nines are often reluctant to lead but can be effective leaders who focus on building consensus. They are often able to simplify complex issues and reassure people under threatening circumstances. They are best in times that call for building harmony or stability; they can bring diverse and conflicting groups and points of view together by finding and clearly articulating common ground. Nines may be less effective in times calling for bold and aggressive action.

When Stressed: Nines can take two approaches to leadership when they are under stress. Their first approach is to become stubborn and cling to ideas and policies that may have outlived their effectiveness. Their second approach is to pass the buck. They may become internally resigned and delegate critical decisions that are their responsibility and absent themselves from important meetings and discussions. Stressed Nines may vacillate between leading dictatorially when consensus is called for and leading by committee when decisiveness is needed.

Influence: wielding effective tactics for persuasion
Typically: Nines persuade by instilling trust in others and from an ability to create an uplifting and positive vision. Because Nines are able to make a personal connection with others, people believe that Nines have their best interest in mind and are willing to hear their point of view. They often prefer to influence from behind the scenes, which makes them appear to lack self-interest. This perceived lack of self-interest makes it easier for them to be persuasive.
When Stressed: Nines may not trust their ability to influence others. They suffer from a lack of self-confidence and question why anyone would want to listen to their point of view. Nines may forget their own significance and the impact they can have on other people.

Conflict Management: Negotiating and resolving disputes
Typically: Nines have a complicated relationship with conflict. In general, they do not enjoy conflict and work hard to avoid it. On the other hand, many Nines enjoy arguments about politics, sports, religion, etc. When faced with conflict, they tend to internally weigh whether or not the conflict is worth the fight. They may react assertively to threats to their autonomy or sense of internal calm, but often avoid other conflict. Nines make great mediators for third-party conflicts because they are able to see all sides of a dispute. They are naturally supportive and make all sides feel that they are being listened to and appreciated.
When Stressed: Nines lose their taste for mediation and withdraw from conflict. They have difficulty setting boundaries and can become overwhelmed. Their attitude of "Do not worry, it will go away or resolve itself" may even make matters worse because they sometimes fail to make necessary interventions. Nines can also become combative and show bursts of anger as their stress increases and they find it more difficult to maintain their inner peacefulness.

The Awareness to Action Process

Improving Initiative

Initiative is an area where many Nines struggle. Unlocking the Nine's full capacity for high performance often lies in improving in this competency. What follows is an example of how a Nine might work on this key developmental area; it is not a literal "cook book" for all Nines, and you may find that improving performance in other competencies is more critical for you. The purpose of this example is to demonstrate how you might use the three steps of The Awareness to Action Process to identify *your* specific developmental areas and improve in those areas

Other competencies that Nines would do well to improve in are Self-Confidence and Adaptability. Initiative, Self-Confidence, and Adaptability are interrelated and improvement in one often facilitates improvement in the other two. Initiative entails the readiness to act on opportunities. Self-confidence includes confidence in one's powers and abilities. Adaptability is the flexibility in handling change. Initiative also includes the self-confidence to take action when no one else sees the need to. Initiative has an impact on adaptability because it also involves being enterprising and willing to change and improvise.

When formulating your own action plan, work on one or two important goals at a time; create small steps that will move you toward each goal; go from easiest to most difficult, and celebrate your success.

Phase One: Build Awareness
Identify a goal:
- Improve performance in the emotional competency of Initiative.

Identify your current patterns.
- "I avoid making decisions, initiating conversations, and making contact. I often prefer to be asked if I want to be involved in things rather than initiating my involvement. While I may be successful in my work and life, it often feels to me and to others that I am holding back just a little bit."

Phase Two: Develop Authenticity

Identify how your Preferred Strategy is in conflict with improving in this competency.

- "To me, Striving to be Peaceful often translates into keeping a low profile by not speaking up in meetings, not "selling" myself or my ideas, and not being assertive or decisive. This behavior helps me feel comfortable, composed, and secure, which reinforces my Striving to be Peaceful, but is in conflict with improving in Initiative"

Revise your strategy so that it incorporates improvement in these competencies. (Remember that when Nines overdo their Striving to be Peaceful they might disregard threats to their security or success and become passive.)

- "True peacefulness lies in addressing problems, tasks, and conflicts now so that my world will be under control and hassle-free in the long run, even if it leads to short-term turmoil. By seizing opportunities, volunteering to take charge of projects, and so forth, I can be more in control of my own fate and avoid problems before they occur."

Phase Three: Take Action

Devise and Execute an Action Plan; be sure that it involves a goal, action steps, a person who will help monitor your success, and a timeline for completion. See Appendix C for a sample Action Plan. Sample action steps are listed below.

- Look for opportunities to act before being asked or forced to.
- Go the extra step and do more than what is expected of you.
- Take charge. Surprise your boss or spouse by expressing exactly what you plan on doing, what time, where, who is going to supply the resources, transportation, etc.
- Be decisive; don't over-analyze everything or hesitate when people ask what you want. Don't always rely on consensus before making a decision.
- Accept the anxiety that you experience when taking the initiative or making changes. It is normal to feel this and you can become comfortable with it. Don't let it stop you from acting. Remember: doing nothing will lead to more disharmony and chaos, not more peacefulness.

- Acknowledge your anger. Rather than repress it, take control of your anger and vent it in appropriate ways. This will head off the very uncontrolled explosions that you fear.
- See Appendix B, General Recommendations for Growth.

EPILOGUE

Your resistance to change is likely to reach its peak when
significant change is imminent.
GEORGE LEONARD

We hope that after reading this book you have identified your personality type and found ways to apply the ideas included here toward improving your performance at work and in other areas of your life.

By way of summary, here are the main concepts to take away from this book:

- Identify your personality type so you can become more conscious of your patterns of thoughts, emotions, and behaviors.
- Decide on what changes you would like to make in your life and set a goal for improvement.
- Modify your preferred strategy so it includes the changes you wish to make.
- Create and implement an action plan.
- Repeat these steps as necessary.

It really is that simple. It is not easy, however. Change requires hard work and consistent effort on your part, and it helps to have support from others. As you begin to apply these steps you will first experience the excitement and joy of learning and growing, but you will inevitably hit a plateau were your progress seems to have stopped, and where nothing seems to be happening.

But we have found that whenever we hit a plateau and ask the question, "Why am I stuck?" the answer is always to be found in the interplay between our Preferred Strategy and Neglected Strategy. For example, when Nines feel unfocused, low on energy, unable to make another sales call, or reluctant to confront someone, you can be sure it is because they're *over using* (and distorting) their Preferred Strategy, S*triving to be Peaceful*, and *under using* (and distorting) their Neglected Strategy, *Striving to be Outstanding.* We have found the same pattern at play for all the types.

Staying aware of this interplay between the preferred and neglected strategies can create the balance required to remain focused on the changes you are trying to make. So when your progress is bogged down, or you are simply in the grips of stress, ask yourself: "How am I over using my Preferred Strategy and under using my Neglected Strategy?" Then repeat the above steps.

171

Over the last decade we have worked with hundreds of clients and seen them effectively apply these principles, and we have applied them to our own lives as well. They work if you are willing to make the effort necessary for growing.

APPENDIX A

The Awareness to Action Emotional Competency Assessment (ECA)

How to Use The Awareness to Action Emotional Competency Assessment

The Awareness to Action Emotional Competency Assessment can be used as a 360-degree assessment or as a self-assessment. Using it as a 360-degree assessment allows you to gather feedback from others; this helps you discover blind spots in your behavior, and involves other people in your performance-improvement process. The following instructions explain how to use the assessment both ways.

Administer the "Other" section of ECA

1. Select five to ten people who will provide honest feedback about your behavior related to the Enneagram Emotional Competencies. These people should be a cross section of boss(es), peers, and direct reports.
2. Distribute the ECA (Other) to the people you have selected to provide the feedback. You can use the Other assessment from this book, but we suggest you request (free of charge) a downloadable pdf file of the *ECA* from www.awarenesstoaction.com.
3. Inform people that you would like them to evaluate your emotional intelligence by completing the assessment.
4. Tell them to be totally honest If they feel they do not know how to rate you on certain items, have them enter a rating of "3".
5. Inform people who receive the assessments that their feedback will be treated anonymously. Your bosses' ratings, of course, are not anonymous to you, but they must be kept confidential.
6. Have people deliver their assessments to you as anonymously as possible.

Complete the "Self" section of The ECA

1. Complete Section A: The ECA (Self).
2. Complete Section C: Build Awareness by comparing scores and setting goals and then entering the Self and Other scores, recording your insights and establishing goals for

173

improvement. Follow the Awareness to Action Process outlined in this book as a guide.

3. Complete Section D: Develop Authenticity.
4. Complete Section E: Take Action. Review Section F: The Enneagram Emotional Competencies Developmental Suggestions for recommendations on improving in your weaker competencies.

Get the Most from ECA

1. You can use The ECA without asking others to participate, but we recommend that you do ask your boss, peers and subordinates to give you feedback. This greatly facilitates the Build Awareness phase of the Awareness to Action Process.
2. Re-read how the Awareness to Action Process works in the chapter related to your type. Understanding how your Preferred Strategy anchors in old behaviors will help you complete the second phase, Develop Authenticity, of the Awareness to Action Process.
3. You will not need to work on all the competencies. If you are like most people, you will be strong in some areas and weak in others, and probably will need to focus on two or three areas. Although the assessment provides space to enter your action steps for the four major competency categories (Self Awareness, Self-Management, Attunement to Others, and Building Relationships), work with the ones that you are the weakest in first.
4. Be as clear as you can about what competencies you need to improve in, how to acquire proficiency in them (see Section F: The Enneagram Emotional Competencies Developmental Suggestions) and how to show it on the job. If you feel comfortable in doing so, ask people who you trust to give you advice on how to improve.
5. Set clear goals. Spell out the specific behaviors and skills that make up your target competencies. Ensure that the goals are clear, specific, and appropriately challenging.
6. Look for opportunities to practice the competencies. Lasting change requires sustained practice on the job and elsewhere in life. An automatic habit, usually related to your preferred strategy, is being unlearned, and unfamiliar behaviors will be practiced. Provide yourself with situations and look for naturally occurring opportunities at work and outside of work to practice the competencies. Practice the new behaviors repeatedly and consistently over a period of months.

174

7. Ask for feedback. *Awareness* is the first step toward change, but don't assume that you are staying on course. Old habits die hard. Ongoing feedback encourages people and directs change. Ask for focused and sustained feedback from people you trust to be honest. Make sure that bosses, peers, subordinates, and even friends and family members give periodic feedback on your progress.

8. The work space provided in this book may not be adequate to enter all of the information you desire. We suggest you use additional paper to expand your insights and action plans. An alternative is to request an expanded version of *The ECA* from www.awarenesstoaction.com.

Section A: The ECA (Self)

Rate the extent to which you feel you display each of the following characteristics by entering the appropriate number (from 1 to 5).

1 = Not at all, 2 = To a small extent, 3 = To some extent,
4 = To a great extent, 5 = To a very great extent

SELF-AWARENESS

1. ____I am aware of my strengths and weaknesses. (Self-Awareness)

2. ____I have an accurate assessment of my own value and contributions. (Self-Awareness)

3. ____I can identify my own feelings, such as anger, frustration, sadness, and anxiety. (Self-Awareness)

4. ____I recognize the effect of my emotions on my performance. (Self-Awareness)

5. ____I am conscious of the effect of my behavior on others. (Self-Awareness)

6. ____I present myself with self-assurance and confidence. (Self-Confidence)

7. ____I am open to feedback, new information and ideas. (Self-Confidence)

8. ____I am committed to continuously learning. (Self-Confidence)

9. ____I am confident in my ability to do my job well. (Self-Confidence)

10. ____I am not afraid to express an unpopular opinion if I believe it is correct. (Self-Confidence)

SELF-AWARENESS TOTAL SCORE: _____

SELF-MANAGEMENT

> **Scale**
> 1 = Not at all, 2 = To a small extent, 3 = To some extent,
> 4 = To a great extent, 5 = To a very great extent

1. ____I can keep disruptive impulses and emotions under control. (Self-Control)

2. ____I can manage my nervousness and anxiety. (Self-Control)

3. ____I am a patient person. (Self-Control)

4. ____I am flexible, can handle change well, and find ways to adapt. (Adaptability)

5. ____I can change my opinion about things. (Adaptability)

6. ____I am consistently honest and trustworthy. (Trustworthiness)

7. ____I stay hopeful and optimistic in the face of disappointments and setbacks. (Optimism)

8. ____I have initiative and act on opportunities. (Initiative)

9. ____I strive to meet or improve standards of excellence. (Achievement Drive)

10. ____I know how to deal with upsetting problems. (Resiliency)

SELF-MANAGEMENT TOTAL SCORE: _____

ATTUNEMENT TO OTHERS

1. ____I care what happens to other people. (Empathy)

2. ____I am sensitive to the feelings of others. (Empathy)

3. ____I respect and tolerate perspectives and opinions that I may not agree with. (Empathy)

4. ____I am good at understanding the way other people feel. (Empathy)

5. ____I can read power relationships and know who is in charge. (Political Awareness)

6. ____I have a good sense of whether people are supporting someone or not. (Political Awareness)

7. ____I can tell who the decision makers are in a group. (Political Awareness)

8. ____I listen openly without interrupting. (Communication)

9. ____I communicate clearly and convincingly. (Communication)

10. ____I ask relevant questions. (Communication)

ATTUNEMENT TOTAL SCORE: _____

RELATIONSHIP BUILDING

1. ____I am able to cultivate and maintain relationships. (Cooperation)

2. ____I strive for mutual understanding and sharing of ideas. (Cooperation)

3. ____I am a team player, and I cooperate and work well with others. (Cooperation)

4. ____I lead by example. (Leadership)

5. ____I am able to take charge, inspire, and lead others to accomplish common goals. (Leadership)

6. ____I am able to persuade people to see my way of thinking. (Influence)

7. ____I send convincing messages and use effective tactics for persuasion. (Influence)

8. ____I use diplomacy manage tense situations and people who don't agree with me. (Conflict Management)

9. ____I am effective in "give and take" discussions, and work toward win-win solutions. (Conflict Management)

10. ____I can effectively negotiate and resolve conflict. (Conflict Management)

RELATIONSHIP TOTAL SCORE: _____

SELF-AWARENESS

This person:

1. _____is aware of his/her strengths and weaknesses. (Self-Awareness)

2. _____has an accurate assessment of his/her own value and contributions. (Self-Awareness)

3. _____can identify his/her own feelings, such as anger, frustration, sadness, anxiety. (Self-Awareness)

4. _____recognizes the effect of his/her emotions on his/her performance. (Self-Awareness)

5. _____is conscious of the effect of his/her behavior on others. (Self-Awareness)

6. _____presents him/her self with self-assurance and confidence. (Self-Confidence)

7. _____is open to feedback, new information, and ideas. (Self-Confidence)

8. _____is committed to continuously learning. (Self-Confidence)

9. _____is confident in his/her ability to do his/her job well. (Self-Confidence)

10. _____is not afraid to express an unpopular opinion if he/she believes it is correct. (Self-Confidence)

SELF-AWARENESS TOTAL SCORE: _____

SELF-MANAGEMENT

> **Scale**
> 1 = Not at all, 2 = To a small extent, 3 = To some extent,
> 4 = To a great extent, 5 = To a very great extent

This person:

1. ____can keep disruptive impulses and emotions under control. (Self-Control)

2. ____can manage his/her nervousness and anxiety. (Self-Control)

3. ____is a patient person. (Self-Control)

4. ____is flexible, can handle change well, and find ways to adapt. (Adaptability)

5. ____can change his/her opinion about things. (Adaptability)

6. ____is consistently honest and trustworthy. (Trustworthiness)

7. ____stays hopeful and optimistic in the face of disappointments and setbacks. (Optimism)

8. ____has initiative and acts on opportunities. (Initiative)

9. ____strives to meet or improve standards of excellence. (Achievement Drive)

10. ____knows how to deal with upsetting problems. (Resiliency)

SELF-MANAGEMENT TOTAL SCORE: _____

ATTUNEMENT TO OTHERS

This person:

1. ____cares what happens to other people. (Empathy)

2. ____is sensitive to the feelings of others. (Empathy)

3. ____respects and tolerates perspectives and opinions that he/she may not agree with. (Empathy)

4. ____is good at understanding the way other people feel. (Empathy)

5. ____can read power relationships and knows who is in charge. (Political Awareness)

6. ____has a good sense of whether people are supporting someone or not. (Political Awareness)

7. ____can tell who the decision makers are in a group. (Political Awareness)

8. ____listens openly without interrupting. (Communication)

9. ____communicates clearly and convincingly. (Communication)

10. ____asks relevant questions. (Communication)

ATTUNEMENT TOTAL SCORE: _____

RELATIONSHIP BUILDING

This person:

1. _____is able to cultivate and maintain relationships. (Cooperation)

2. _____strives for mutual understanding and sharing of ideas. (Cooperation)

3. _____is a team player and cooperates and works well with others. (Cooperation)

4. ____ leads by example. (Leadership)

5. _____is able to take charge, inspire, and lead others to accomplish common goals. (Leadership)

6. ____ is able to persuade people to see his/her way of thinking. (Influence)

7. _____sends convincing messages and uses effective tactics for persuasion. (Influence)

8. _____uses diplomacy to manage tense situations and people who don't agree with him/her. (Conflict Management)

9. _____is effective in "give and take" discussions, and works toward win-win solutions. (Conflict Management)

10. _____can effectively negotiate and resolve conflict. (Conflict Management)

RELATIONSHIP TOTAL SCORE: _____

Section C: Build Awareness

Self-Awareness: *Self* Score:_____ *Other* Score:_____
What is your goal? (Which competencies are you trying to improve?)

What are your current behaviors identified by you and by others?

What insights and conclusions have you learned from comparing the Self and Other scores?

Self-Management: *Self* Score:_____ *Other* Score:_____
What is your goal? (Which competencies are you trying to improve?)

What are your current behaviors identified by you and by others?

What insights and conclusions have you learned from comparing the Self and Other scores?

Attunement to Others: *Self* Score:_____ *Other* Score:_____
What is your goal? (Which competencies are you trying to improve?)

What are your current behaviors identified by you and by others?

What insights and conclusions have you learned from comparing the Self and Other scores?

Relationship Building: *Self* Score:_____ *Other* Score:_____
What is your goal? (Which competencies are you trying to improve?)

What are your current behaviors identified by you and by others?

What insights and conclusions have you learned from comparing the Self and Other scores?

Section D: Develop Authenticity

Self-Awareness: How is your Preferred Strategy in conflict with improving in this competency?

Revise your strategy so that it incorporates improvement in this competency.

Self-Management: How is your Preferred Strategy in conflict with improving in this competency?

Revise your strategy so that it incorporates improvement in this competency.

Attunement to Others: How is your Preferred Strategy in conflict with improving in this competency?

Revise your strategy so that it incorporates improvement in this competency.

Relationship Building: How is your Preferred Strategy in conflict with improving in this competency?

Revise your strategy so that it incorporates improvement in this competency.

Section E: Take Action

Self-Awareness: Create and Execute an Action Plan; be sure that it involves a goal, action steps, a person who will help monitor your success, and a timeline for completion. See Appendix C for a Sample Action Plan.

Self-Management: Create and Execute an Action Plan; be sure that it involves a goal, action steps, a person who will help monitor your success, and a timeline for completion. See Appendix C for a Sample Action Plan.

Attunement to Others: Create and Execute an Action Plan; be sure that it involves a goal, action steps, a person who will help monitor your success, and a timeline for completion. See Appendix C for a Sample Action Plan.

Relationship Building: Create and Execute an Action Plan; be sure that it involves a goal, action steps, a person who will help monitor your success, and a timeline for completion. See Appendix C for a Sample Action Plan.

Section F: The Enneagram Emotional Competency Developmental Suggestions

PERSONAL COMPETENCIES

Self-Awareness

Self-Awareness: ability to identify one's thought processes, emotions, and skills

To improve in this competency:

- Become aware of your strengths and weaknesses by asking for feedback.
- Gain a realistic view of your values and contributions: don't over or under estimate them.
- Become conscious of the effect of your behavior by asking what impact your verbal, written, and nonverbal actions have on people. Ask people how your behavior makes them feel.
- Inquire within about which emotions you are feeling and why, for example, "Why am I feeling anxious? What event caused It? How am I reacting to it?"
- Recognize how your emotions affect your performance both negatively and positively. For example, does feeling frustrated cause you to make irrational decisions, or does feeling angry move you to take decisive action?
- Discover your "blind spots" through feedback. Explore how your thinking process, and your internal filters, prejudices and preferences affect your actions.

Self-Confidence: confidence in one's powers and abilities
To improve in this competency:

- Present yourself in a self-assured, calm manner.
- Express confidence in your ability to do a good job.
- Have the courage to express an unpopular opinion if you believe it is correct.
- When appropriate, step up and take command of situations.
- Be more decisive and get comfortable making decisions under pressure.
- Model a "can do" attitude. Understand and solve problems instead of focusing on why things can't be done.

Self-Management

Self-Control: restraint exercised over one's impulses, emotions, or desires
To improve in this competency:

- Be patient. Whether your impulse is fight, flight, or freeze, take a moment to think through your actions.
- Build up a tolerance for discomfort; whether this means resisting the urge to withdraw or the urge to attack, learn to tolerate the tension.
- Resist distraction from your most important activities. Engage in a daily battle with procrastination. Prioritize the work and identify what's important, urgent, etc. Focus on the important.
- Count to ten, relax, and manage your nervousness and anxiety.
- When under stress, focus on the task at hand, concentrate and think clearly.
- Handle hostile or disruptive people without escalating the hostility.

Adaptability: flexibility in handling change
To improve in this competency:

- Don't underestimate your ability to change; instead, remember past successes in handling change, and find ways to adapt to changing circumstances.
- Be open to changing your opinion when given new, convincing data.
- Adapt your reactions and responses to fit the situation and the person. Be flexible in the way you perceive and interpret circumstances and people.
- Expect that your work environment is dynamic and chaotic, not consistent and stable. With this expectation you can scan the horizon for possible changes, identify them early, reduce surprise, and take a proactive stance toward expected changes.
- When you first encounter shifting priorities and change, don't react. Gain more information before you express your reaction. Internalizing the change may make it easier for you to accept.
- View shifting priorities and other changes as new challenges or opportunities to think creatively. Be confident you will be

188

able to brainstorm ways to get around any obstacles the change presents.

Trustworthiness: maintaining standards of honesty and integrity
To improve in this competency:
- Be consistently honest and trustworthy.
- Understand the difference between "spinning" facts and telling the truth.
- Behave ethically and consistently be true to your own values.
- Be a "real person" who makes mistakes, talks about them, shares solutions, and asks for help from others.
- Remember that actions speak louder than words. Consistently engage in solid ethical behavior and confront any unethical practices.
- Don't make commitments you can't keep. Make realistic time and resource estimates based on your previous experience. If you have not had experience in an area, ask someone who has such experience to give you estimates, and then add time for the initial learning curve.

Optimism: ability to anticipate and expect the best possible outcome
To improve in this competency:
- Stay hopeful in the face of disappointments and setbacks.
- Function out of an anticipation of success rather than a fear of failure.
- Perceive setbacks as a result of normal, manageable events rather than due to personal shortcomings.
- Look for the good in people or situations before you look for the bad.
- Look for the good in yourself and make a conscious choice to be positive.
- Learn from your mistakes and trust that your actions can have a positive effect on others.

Initiative: readiness to act on opportunities
To improve in this competency:
- Stretch yourself and work at a level beyond what is expected.
- Do what it takes to get the job done, including cutting through bureaucracy.
- Refrain from saying, "it can't be done," and focus on how you can make it happen.

189

- Bring people and resources together to capitalize on opportunities.
- Think "outside the box." Remember that one person's attic is another person's e-Bay gold mine.
- "Take the shot" when the opportunity arises. You will occasionally miss, but that you will *never* hit the goal if you are not ready and willing to shoot for it.

Achievement Drive: striving to meet or improve a standard of excellence
To improve in this competency:
- Set challenging goals and work aggressively toward accomplishing them.
- On a regular basis, monitor your performance as it relates to your standards. Does it meet the criteria for exceptional performance?
- Be willing to measure yourself against external standards ("the competition") and internal standards (your personal goals and values) and strive toward excellence in both.
- Up the ante: continually strive to improve your performance.
- Respectfully challenge the status quo. Constantly ask why things are done the way they are currently being done.
- Seek out feedback about how well you are doing.

Resiliency: capacity to endure in the face of obstacles
To improve in this competency:
- Deal with upsetting problems appropriately, without over- or under-reacting, and recover rapidly from stress.
- Recognize the difference between failure and calling yourself a failure.
- Understand errors. When you attempt something and fail, ask yourself, "What have I learned?" rather than kick yourself or blame someone else. Discovering the value in your mistakes will make you a better, smarter person.
- Be challenged rather than threatened by other people.
- Consider a setback or rejection as a learning experience. Review the events that led up to it, and access your attitude and behavior at the time. Identify what you did well and what you might have done differently.
- Embrace the idea that a life without challenges is not much of a life,

Attunement to Others

Empathy: *awareness of and participation in others' feelings, ideas, and needs*

To improve in this competency:

- Care what happens to other people and take an active interest in their needs and ideas. Be sensitive to the feelings of others. Listen closely, be aware of emotional cues, ask people how they are doing, and how you can help.
- Assume that people are operating from good motives and give people the benefit of the doubt.
- Respect and tolerate perspectives and opinions that you may not agree with.
- "Walk a mile in my shoes:" Consistently try to understand the way other people feel. Treat other people as they want to be treated, not as *you* want to be treated.
- Confront issues, not people, and allow people to save face.
- Minimize sarcasm. Remind yourself that your goal is to retain your sense of humor while avoiding any tendencies to insult or hurt others. If you offend people, analyze the way in which you misused your wit— and apologize.

Political Awareness: *reading a group's emotional currents and power relationships*

To improve in this competency:

- Study, inquire, and ask for information in order to realistically perceive organizational dynamics.
- Understand how (and which) people, elements, and events influence the views of people and organizations.
- Try to read power relationships and know who is in charge.
- Work to acquire a good sense of which ideas have the group's support.
- Ask questions and listen attentively. Try to perceive who the decision makers are in a group, verify your perception and learn from it.
- Stay in touch with well-informed people.

Communication: *listening openly and sending convincing messages*

To improve in this competency:

191

- Encourage open dialogue and accept bad as well as good news.
- Effectively use emotions, tone of voice, and nonverbal communication to convey your message.
- Listen openly without interrupting.
- Paraphrase discussions to ensure that your perceptions are accurate.
- Communicate clearly and convincingly.
- Attempt to keep people as informed as possible. Ask yourself: Am I withholding information that others need? Do I allow time to address questions and problems? Do I give people only the information they need?

Relationship Building

Cooperation: working with others toward shared goals
To improve in this competency:
- Make it a priority to cultivate and maintain relationships. Encourage cooperation, rather than competition, between different work units. Willingly share resources, ideas, and support. Make sure groups set their goals in harmony with one another and that the goals are mutually supportive.
- Build into your working relationships with people an agreement that mutual, constructive criticism will be the norm, not the exception.
- Help people understand one another better. Share information about how work is being done. Discuss work histories, specific skills, success, and talents.
- Help team members to understand, appreciate, and use differences among themselves to arrive at better solutions and to do better work.
- Encourage everyone to speak a common language. To avoid alienating outside groups, educate them and help them to understand the "lingo" of the team.
- Foster an environment of trust by ensuring all criticism is constructive and is focused on individuals' behaviors.

Leadership: inspiring and leading individuals and groups
To improve in this competency:
- Lead by example. Walk your talk, and don't expect anyone to do more than you do or to be more committed than you.

- Inspire, coach, and monitor the performance of others while holding them accountable for their performance.
- Clearly describe your vision and inspire others to share it. Don't expect people to know what your vision is: keep repeating it with passion, confidence, and faith.
- Lead without pretense. The secret of strong leadership is not to appear all-powerful and all-knowing. Keep in mind the proverb: "It is my imperfections that endear me to my friends. It is my virtues that annoy them."
- Inspire and motivate people by expressing every positive feeling that crosses your mind, and when you must be negative, balance it with lots of good strokes.
- Be rigorous about your personal values and standards. Understand that leaders need followers, and people will follow a leader they like and admire, not a leader they despise and mistrust. Treat people in a way that makes them want to follow you.

Influence: wielding effective tactics for persuasion
To improve in this competency:
- Know how to create and present yourself and your message in the most appealing manner. Make your point in dramatic and memorable ways.
- Have a strong network that can help build consensus through direct and indirect influence.
- Understand the culture, goals, obstacles, financial restrictions, and aspirations of your audience. Have complete knowledge of your subject, be a masterful communicator, and express your message with confidence.
- Determine whether you have the information necessary to accomplish the task at hand. If not, decide on what you need to know and how you can get the information.
- When a decision is important to other people, find out what they think you should consider before deciding.
- Listen carefully to peoples' input; it will give you their understanding of the issue, their rationale for their opinion, the conclusion or decision they want to reach—and effective ways to influence them.

Conflict Management: negotiating and resolving disputes
To improve in this competency:

- Deliberately look at issues from the viewpoint of different constituencies.
- Be concerned if you are reluctant or unable to understand the viewpoint of others. This reaction is an important warning signal, because it will be difficult for you to manage or resolve conflict well if you cannot, at least partially, understand the other point of view.
- Consider alternative solutions instead of going with the first option that presents itself. There may be more alternatives than you imagine.
- Encourage open discussion and feedback.
- Foresee potential conflicts, bring them into the open, and help resolve them. Encourage give and take discussions, and negotiate win-win solutions.
- Practice the "The Stoplight Approach:"

Red Light	1. Stop, calm down, and think before you act.
Yellow Light	2. Describe the problem and how you feel.
	3. Set a positive goal.
	4. Think of lots of solutions.
	5. Think ahead to the consequences.
Green Light	6. Go ahead and try the best plan.

APPENDIX B

General Recommendations for Growth

There are many tried and true recommendations for each of the types. Some may apply to you and some may not. Reviewing these may trigger an insight on how you may further improve your performance.

General Recommendations for Ones

- *Recognize your inner critic.* Be aware of how you criticize yourself and how this criticism is not fixing things, as you might think, but is really the source of much of your anger and frustration. Your inner critic is not the voice of God or the voice of reason. Tell your inner critic to "bug off" and take a vacation from self-criticism.
- *Relax.* Don't demand so much from yourself. Being a workaholic leads to mistakes, frustration, and tension—not perfection.
- *Learn to give ground, cooperate, and compromise.* Resist digging in your heels and insisting that things be done your way simply for the sake of honor. Practice being reasonable and pragmatic and give up rigidity and stubbornness.
- *Accept that things are never "perfect" in your eyes.* This attitude can cause indecision and procrastination because you fear making mistakes. Learn what "good enough" is, stop "tweaking" things, and take action.
- *Resist criticizing others.* When you feel you must take a stand, or when you find yourself having a disagreement, speak non-judgmentally. Try to see the other point of view, and look for the gray areas.

General Recommendations for Twos

- *Accept that not everyone will like you, nor do they need to.* Be aware of how much time you spend trying to win people over through flattery, helpful hints, advice, and so forth.
- *Do some activities alone.* Practice independent activities that force you to take the lead or to work outside of the team. You do not have to work through others or get your needs met

195

through others. Autonomy is not as uncomfortable as you may suspect.

- *Recognize the importance of being task-oriented, as well as people-oriented.* Dot your "i's" and cross your "t's." You get paid to produce measurable results, not to nurture people.
- *Be direct and learn to accept what part you play in interpersonal conflicts.* Expecting special treatment and feeling that people should meet your needs without your needing to ask them is at the root of many of your conflicts. Anticipating that people will read your mind is a poor communication skill and a blueprint for problems.
- *Be honest with yourself about your real motives.* Recognize how much of your behavior is motivated by the desire to be recognized and praised.

General Recommendations for Threes

- *Find balance in your life.* If you are to achieve all that you desire and are capable of you need to find a fuller and more balanced way of living.
- *Slow down.* Resist the temptation to bring closure quickly so that you can move on to the next challenge. Be aware that fixing problems later is a lot more burdensome, expensive, and impractical than taking the time to do it right the first time.
- *Resist cutting corners.* Don't compromise on quality by using inferior facilities, ingredients, etc.
- *Be clear about what you can accomplish.* Don't over promise for the sake of looking good or making a sale. Develop realistic job expectations; don't inflate your abilities or accomplishments.
- *Admit to your mistakes.* Have the courage to confront your own inauthentic behavior when it occurs.

General Recommendations for Fours

- *See what part envy plays in your life.* How much energy do you spend entertaining negative, even vengeful, thoughts about co-workers? Channel that energy to improving your own performance, and forget about what "great" jobs, bosses, or lives other people have.

196

- *Learn to collaborate with others.* Let "ordinary" people and experiences influence you.
- *Stop over dramatizing.* When you feel strong emotions coming over you, ask yourself if you can control them. Count to ten before expressing strong feelings—especially when they are negative.
- *Don't linger too long on fantasy, the past, and the pain you've felt.* Quite often the best thing you can do is to *get up and get moving.* Exercise can help you move out of negative moods, as can being with people in a social setting.
- *Don't expect someone to save you.* It is OK to expect that people be there for you, but be conscious of whether you expect or even demand that they take care of you. Don't look for special treatment.

General Recommendations for Fives

- *Learn to collaborate with others.* Create alignments with people who can help you get your ideas implemented.
- *Stop preparing for life and start living it.* You probably have more than enough information to begin, continue, or finish a project. Just do it!
- *Don't minimize your needs.* Ask for what you need, especially in relationships with your boss and coworkers. Express your thoughts and feelings and trust that people will accept them and you. Don't withdraw and assume that people can read your mind. They can't.
- *Come down to earth.* Devoting time to acquiring impractical knowledge will do little for your career when you should be developing interpersonal skills and building relationships.
- *Develop your people skills.* Enlist someone at work to be your "emotional mentor"—to help you learn to read the emotional reactions of others. Get to know people personally by asking if they've seen any good movies, how their families are doing, how their weekend was, and so forth.

General Recommendations for Sixes

- *Trust your own judgment and experience.* Avoid believing that some authority, system, or company has more insight into what you need.

197

- *Stop complaining and blaming.* Try to see the negative effect these have on your work and relationships. Take action rather than bemoan things.
- *Focus on what you* want—your goals—not on what you *don't want,* and stop obsessing about what could go wrong.
- *Draw on your own skills and competence.* Take the initiative and be proactive rather than be reactive.
- *Take a deep breath.* When you are frozen by doubt or indecision, remember to breathe, and breathe deeply, then take action. Remind yourself that being uncertain is normal, and need not affect you so negatively. Remember that your fear does not have to completely disappear before you can act.

General Recommendations for Sevens

- *Stay focused.* Don't distract yourself from painful experiences or try to chase away unpleasant feelings so quickly. Let yourself feel and process them and find out what is behind them; ultimately this will relieve the anxiety you are trying to avoid.
- *Tell the truth.* Be conscious of how you "spin" stories to make them more exciting or eventful, and how you "reframe" mistakes or offensive behavior to avoid being held responsible for your behavior.
- *Do your own work.* Finish the details and legwork rather than pass it on to others. Don't rely on your charm, humor or ability to "BS" to get people to do the "dirty work."
- *Follow through.* Don't let projects go unfinished or commitments go unmet.
- *Become comfortable with silence.* Being detached from hyperactive behavior or frenetic activity does not mean being dull, or empty, although you may see it that way at first. Practice keeping your focus on the present rather than in the future.

General Recommendations for Eights

- *Accept the fact that you can't always get what you want.*
- *Identify people and situations that trigger your anger and loss of control.* Rehearse mentally how you will control your behavior before encountering them.
- *Get help.* Have a co-worker—preferably someone whose self-control you admire—watch you and quietly say "patience," or some agreed upon code word or signal when he sees you about to lose control.
- *Solicit feedback.* Sincerely ask for feedback from coworkers about how your impulsiveness affects them. Remember not to kill the messenger.
- *Be patient.* Accept the fact that people don't speak or act as quickly as you would like them to. Let people finish their thoughts and then, just to be sure, internally count to five before taking your turn to talk.

General Recommendations for Nines

- *Finish what you start and take credit for what you do.* Don't minimize your contributions and accomplishments or credit others for what you do.
- *Find your own position.* Question whether you are adopting someone else's philosophy to avoid being confrontational or making a decision. Believe in and express your ideas.
- *Ask for what you need and want without reservation*—and believe that you are important enough to get what you want.
- *Address conflict directly.* Stop treating people as if they were fragile and can't handle your assertiveness; they can, and will usually welcome your directness.
- *Become engaged.* Exercise regularly to become aware of your body and emotions. Exert yourself and embrace your own importance. Be wakeful, conscious, and willing to risk being truly alive.

Appendix C

Creating an Action Plan

A new pattern of behavior is more likely to be successful when:
- The desired behavior and skill is clearly defined.
- There is a motivation to change.
- Sources of resistance are identified.
- There are specific activities aimed at facilitating the change.
- Other people are involved in supporting the change.
- The outcomes are visible.

Some additional things to think about:
- Direct your efforts toward a single behavior or a related set of behaviors.
- Keep your plan simple.
- Put your plan in writing. Writing it down helps focus your mind clarifies the plan and solidifies your commitment to taking the appropriate steps.
- Discuss your plan with co-workers and people who will encourage you.

Action Plan Instructions

I. *Area to Be Developed:* record what competency or behavior you want to improve.

II. *Benefits to You, Your Team, Your Organization*: list the personal and/or professional benefits to you, your team, and/or your organization.

III. *Barriers and Strategies for Success:* record the barriers that could hinder your success. Some may be interior (lack of education or training, old habits, attitudes, etc.); others may be external (team structure or composition, company culture, demands on your time and energy, policies and procedures, etc.). List your strategy or action to overcome these barriers. Consider things you can: *stop doing* (old counterproductive habits), *start doing* (new effective behaviors), and *continue doing* (using current strengths more effectively).

IV. *Action Steps and Time Frame:* list an activity within a specific time frame for each action step. Plan for how you will overcome specific barriers to the completion of each action step.

V. *Involvement of Others:* record the people you want to help you and the specific help you want from them. Getting other people involved, whether through providing training, feedback, or encouragement will help you stay focused and motivated.

VI. *Showing Progress:* for each action step in section IV, list how you will know you have made progress toward the changes identified in section I.

Action Plan

I. *Area to Be Developed:*

II. *Benefits to You, Your Team, Your Organization:*

III. *Barriers and Strategies for Success:*

IV. *Action Steps and Time Frame:*

V. *Involvement of Others:*

VI. *Showing Progress:*

Appendix D

Identifying Type

As we said in Chapter Three, identifying your personality type and the type of others can be difficult.

Identifying one's own personality type is difficult because we see both so much of ourselves and so little of ourselves at the same time. We are constantly bombarded by inner thoughts and drives, and these sometimes conflict with each other. It is part of the human condition that we don't see ourselves as objectively as we think we do. Therefore, we may not see the habitual patterns of behavior that others may see in us. More likely than not, we will see ourselves in three or four of the different personality types.

Identifying someone else's personality type can be difficult because all we see are the external results—what they say and do rather than what their thoughts and motivations may be. We may see certain behaviors and assume that they are a given personality type because we've seen people of that type display those behaviors before. (For example, we may see someone who is particularly fastidious about grammar and assume they are a Type One because we've seen other Ones who are similarly fastidious.) A particular behavior or trait, however, will not determine a person's Enneagram personality type.

Remember, as was explained in Chapter One, there is a significant difference between strategies and traits. This model of personality is based on habitual preference for one of nine "strategies" or approaches to the world. People who share the same preferred strategy will tend to demonstrate similar behaviors and traits, but this doesn't mean that *only* people of that type will display certain traits.

Therefore, when trying to determine your own personality type, it is critical to consider not just *what* you do, but *why* you do it. It is also important to use great caution when trying to determine someone else's personality type because, while you may be able to

203

observe traits over time, it is difficult to understand the inner workings of another's mind. In other words, you may see the actions but you may not understand the strategy behind those actions.

With that caveat, we have identified some work-related behavioral patterns that may be useful in identifying your type. In nearly a decade of coaching executives, we have observed specific "derailers" that tend to undermine the performance of each of the types. These derailers are strategy-related; that is, they occur when the stress and challenges of work interact with the preferred strategy for approaching one's world. This interaction results in a pattern of behavior that may not seem like a problem to the individual but it derails their performance. For example, Seven's tendency to "avoid unpleasantness" makes perfect sense to the Seven, but they can be blinded to how it undermines their ability to confront problems and resolve conflict.

If you are still not sure of your personality type, review the lists of derailers below. If you see yourself in one of them, it may indicate that you are that type.

Derailers for the Nine Personality Types

Type One Derailers
- *Meritocracy:* The belief that people should be judged solely on "merit" (being right; working harder than others; scoring well on exams; accomplishing tasks on deadline; etc), rather than on things like political connection, likeability, etc.
- *Unwillingness to change:* Belief that, since "I am right," others should change, no matter who tells me I'm wrong or that I am the one that needs to change behavior.
- *Seeing the world in black and white:* Too much focus on right and wrong; inability, or unwillingness, to see life as complex and situational; unwillingness to bend or compromise.
- *Not having fun:* Being too "serious;" unwilling to relax and be light-hearted; maintaining a stiff and detached façade.

- *Perfectionism:* Inability to let go of a decision, project, or assignment until the solution is perfect; focus on the mistakes of others rather than positive accomplishments.
- *Always being right:* Conviction that your solution is the only correct solution combined with defensiveness about your position. Seeing suggestions and alternatives as affronts to your position rather than being open-minded and looking for ways that your position can be enhanced.

Type Two Derailers

- *Breaking boundaries:* The desire to "help" causes you to become intrusive and involve yourself in the affairs of others, whether invited or not.
- *Histrionics:* Inappropriate and overly-emotional responses to circumstances; can be excessive displays of anger, sadness, jealousy, excitement, etc.
- *Playing favorites:* Seeing some people as more worthy of your attention than others; an innate tendency to rank others by perceived value and treat them accordingly. This can also lead to abrupt treatment of people or issues that you do not see as important.
- *Worrying about everyone else's problems:* Focusing on the needs and desires of other people instead of your own in an effort to be helpful and appreciated.
- *Needing other people to like you:* Anxiety, conformity, self-sacrifice, and/or insincerity caused by the need to have other people like you.
- *Always taking support role:* Resistance to leading from the front; preferring to lead from behind by advising, supporting, or manipulating.

Type Three Derailers

- *Spin and wanting to look good:* The tendency to put the best possible face on things or events, which at times involves
- leaving out of less attractive facts, can cause lack of trust from others.

- *Taking on too much (the "I'll do it" syndrome):* Desire to be highly accomplished and seen as adding value leads to taking on too many projects.
- *Not seeming "knowable":* Trying to be all things to all people leads to being unknown to all; having no "nooks and crannies" means that others sometimes perceive you as being superficial.
- *Seeking recognition:* Compulsively bringing attention to your accomplishments and importance.
- *The Individual Contributor syndrome:* Seeing other people as impediments who often slow down your progress and ability to accomplish your goals; failure to nurture subordinates because you prefer to "lead by example."

Type Four Derailers
- *Rebellion for rebellion's sake:* Anger at not feeling "special" causes you to act out and rebel against sources of authority and the status quo.
- *Making it different:* Desire to be seen as unique causes you to separate your way of doing things from the way that everyone else does things, whether this adds value or not. This sometimes means you make things more complicated than they need to be.
- *Insistence on being right:* Insistence on being right; defensiveness about position; hostile negativity toward other opinions or ways of doing things.
- *Drama:* Excessive displays of emotion; often making problems and slights out to be greater than they really are.
- *Resentment:* Hostility toward and downplaying of accomplishments of others; feeling that you are not appreciated for your special qualities and others are getting all the credit or lucky breaks.

Type Five Derailers
- *Thinking too much, doing too little:* Preferring analysis to action and allowing that preference to affect performance.
- *Not nurturing relationships:* Neglecting to make contact with others and identify needs; avoidance of networking and social connection.

- *Unaware of your surroundings and your own impact:* Constant inward focus leads to not noticing the effects of your actions (or lack of action) on those around you.
- *Needing to show off intellect:* Showing off knowledge; too much attention to detail, talking too much in areas of expertise; "know-it-all-ism."
- *Not sharing information:* Not communicating with others either through neglect or because you simply don't want to share.

Type Six Derailers
- *Pessimism:* Focusing on problems rather then solutions; looking for what could go wrong rather than what could go right; includes complaining.
- *Suspicion:* Doubt about the good will of others' motives and agenda.
- *Holding back:* Fear of taking risks and resistance to assuming leadership and authority.
- *Indecisiveness:* Inability to settle on one course of action or to trust that your decision is the correct one. Will sometimes use combativeness to feel certain.
- *Combativeness:* Instinctively taking the devil's advocate role; hostility toward change and "outsiders."
- *The "Dog with a Bone" Syndrome:* Relentless persistence in making your point of view heard and winning approval for your ideas.

Type Seven Derailers
- *Talking too much:* Dominating conversations; reluctance to listen to others or ask probing questions; expressing uncensored thoughts to fill conversational voids.
- *Not following through:* Tendency to start the next project before the current one is finished.
- *Hyperactivity and impulsiveness:* Taking action before thinking things through; impatience; nervous activity that makes others uncomfortable.
- *Avoiding Unpleasantness:* Failing to address or absenting yourself from unpleasant people, situations, or tasks.

- *Always wanting more:* Never being satisfied with what you currently have; looking for additional compensation, recognition, or reward; always looking to the next "treat."

Type Eight Derailers
- *Bullying:* Verbally abusing co-workers, often in the guise of "tough love" or "straight talk," sometimes in an attempt to be helpful and sometimes for your own amusement.
- *Volatility and Overwhelming others:* Overwhelming others with anger or the intensity of your opinions; aggressively pushing your agenda; focus on task at the expense of feelings.
- *Always being right:* Arrogance and unwillingness to hear feedback or other points of view.
- *Needing to be the boss:* An overwhelming need to be in charge, or at least feel like you are in charge.
- *Rough around the edges:* Cultivating a coarseness of manner; getting enjoyment out of shocking people; rebelling against the status quo.
- *Impatience and impulsiveness:* Unwillingness to delay action or decisions; expecting others to act at your pace.

Type Nine Derailers
- *Holding back:* Unwillingness to assert yourself fully out of self-doubt or fear of appearing arrogant.
- *Avoiding conflict:* Letting conflict or potential conflict fester unaired and unresolved.
- *Passive aggressiveness:* Getting your way through inaction; punishing others or proving points indirectly; stating uncomfortable comments through sarcasm or "humor."
- *Fuzzy around agreements and details:* Conveniently forgetting unpleasant details; relying on non-affirmative responses to signal negatives.
- *Losing temper:* Letting unresolved conflicts and unexpressed anger build to a volcanic climax.
- *The Nice Guy Syndrome:* Seeming to lack the killer instinct and high self-regard often looked for in leaders.

Appendix E

Applying the Enneagram of Strategies to Other Competency Models

After the first version of this book was published, clients began to ask us about how our personality model could be applied to competency models in addition to the emotional competencies.

This is very simple to do once you understand the concept of the Strategies. This appendix describes how we did it for a leadership model and a sales model.

We took very different approaches in developing these applications, partially based on our clients' needs and partially based on an ethical concern about the potential appearance of "ranking" the nine types in a specific leadership model. Since this model was used in the organization's performance appraisal process (and thus affected advancement within the company), we agreed to focus on why *each* type might potentially go off track in each of the competencies and how to get them back on track. This is a more neutral approach than focusing on which types will be strong and which will be weak in the competencies of the leadership model.

The Strategies and Leadership Competencies

Many organizations are creating leadership competency models in an effort to gain a competitive advantage in the marketplace.

It works like this: Leadership is both critical and complicated. In order to help their people become better leaders companies must create some sort of metrics—measurable competencies that it can communicate to its staff. The competencies are grouped into a model or logical construct so they can be remembered easily. Some organizations create their own leadership competency models, others use a generic competency model developed by someone else.

Often, the model has some relevance to the company's industry and is based on "best practices." For example, a company will dispatch either internal or external consultants to identify what factors lead to success in a particular environment—say, high-tech or financial services, for example—and then create a model based on those factors. A company in an industry where empathy is a useful quality—such as health care or education—will usually include empathy in its leadership competency model; a high-tech company, however, will focus on competencies such as intellect or speed of execution.

Other times, the competency model will be based on the personal philosophy of the powers that be in a company. One such model is the well-known "4-E (and 1-P)" framework advocated by Jack Welch, retired CEO of General Electric. Many other companies have adopted this model or a slightly revised version of it, including a client company that we will refer to as International Software Technologies (IST).

According to Welch's book, "Winning," the 4-E's and 1-P are:

- Positive *Energy*—the ability to thrive on action and relish change.
- *Energize*—the ability to get others revved up.
- *Edge*—the courage to make tough yes-or-no decisions.
- *Execute*—the ability to get the job done.
- *Passion* —heartfelt, deep excitement about work.

Welch used this framework when making hiring and organizational design decisions, feeling that if his executives didn't have these qualities they would struggle to be successful at GE.

While the authors have never met Jack Welch or consulted with GE, it is not a stretch to believe that Welch is an Eight and probably liked to surround himself with other Eights. In fact, the 4-E and 1-P framework seems like a recipe for manufacturing Eights, were such a thing possible.

IST altered Welch's framework slightly to reflect the needs of its organizational culture. The model became:

- *Envision*—identify meaningful and innovative change that produces profitable growth.
- *Energize*—which combines Welch's "positive energy" and "energize."
- *Edge*—cuts to the essence of what is important.
- *Execute*—achieves results better and faster than the competition.
- *Values*—is ethical always and everywhere.

(*Note*—these are abbreviated definitions of the terms and IST has delineated subcategories under each competency.)

These changes demonstrate an interesting difference in the cultures of the two companies; GE has traditionally seemed Eight-ish in its culture while IST has a One-ish culture.

What follows are descriptions of how the Enneagram was used to help two coaching clients become more effective in terms of

210

IST's leadership competency model. These examples are based on composites rather than on any specific client.

Case 1: Alice M., vice-president of marketing, Type Eight.

At Alice's annual review she was given feedback from Paul, her boss and the General Manager of the sector, that rather than being deficient in any of the competencies, she has too much "Edge." Specifically, she tends to exhibit classic Eight-ish behaviors at work—she is blunt and, at times, insensitive when she communicates to others. She can be impatient with her subordinates, becoming easily frustrated when they do not understand things as quickly as she does or when their reports are not exactly how she expects them to be. In meetings she tends to dominate the conversations, cutting people off, subtly denigrating other points of view, and becoming dismissive of those who she believes are not intelligent or experienced enough.

Paul also told Alice that she sometimes has shows a tendency to "over-Execute;" that is, she may act before thinking through all of the consequences of her actions.

"Sometimes you need to let things sit for another day or so before you act," said Paul.

Alice had a difficult time believing that one could have "too much Edge" or "over-Execute," but since she wanted to continue to advance in her career she was willing to work with an executive coach.

Alice misuses the strategies in the way that most Eights do:
1. She tends to overdo striving to be powerful and becomes bossy, impatient, overwhelming, etc.
2. She underutilizes striving to be connected, fearing that reaching out to others or being "too nice" will make her seem weak or dependent.
3. She sometimes misuses detachment in service of power, causing her to seem aloof and insensitive.

Given these dynamics, it is easy to see why Alice can fall into the trap of having too much edge and over-executing.

When she saw the patterns herself, Alice decided to start making some changes. Working with her coach, she started to explore her preferred strategy, focusing on the ways that her desire to be powerful allowed her to justify her tendencies to be overly blunt, impatient, insensitive, etc.

"For me, 'power' is about getting things done, whatever the cost," Alice said. "These behaviors I was being criticized for seemed appropriate in the context of 'getting things done.' What I didn't realize before was that my 'Edge' was not merely focused on business challenges, it was cutting down the very people I needed to help me meet those challenges."

211

Alice began to see true "power" as the ability to work effectively with and through other people, and that this required cooperation rather than commanding, communicating rather than directing, and building people up rather than knocking them down.

As Alice worked with her preferred strategy—striving to be powerful—her application of her neglected and support strategies improved as well. She didn't automatically see emotionally connecting with people as weakness and dependence and she learned to balance her detachment, using it when she was required to make tough decisions but not being insensitive to the needs and feelings of the people around her.

Alice made quick progress, but old habits don't simply disappear and she would sometimes find herself slipping into old behaviors—especially under stress. She kept focusing on these simple issues, however, and she is back on the fast-track for advancement.

Case 2: Paul S., general manager, Type Nine.

Paul, Alice's boss, received feedback from the CEO that he also had a problem with "Edge."

"I'm not quite sure what it is, Paul," said Tom. "Sometimes you don't show enough Edge; other times you slice people apart with it. You can be vague, indirect, and aloof in some circumstances; then you lash out and cut people down at the knees.

"You need to get a handle on this if you want to continue to advance."

Paul knew he had these contradictory tendencies but didn't know quite how to solve the problem so he, too, engaged an executive coach.

Paul misuses the strategies in the same way that other Nines do:

1. He tends to overdo striving to be peaceful and sometimes becomes conflict-averse, vague, and aloof.
2. He underutilizes striving to be outstanding, become overly self-deprecating so he is not seen as arrogant or self-important.
3. He sometimes uses striving to be secure in service of peacefulness, avoiding situations and people who make him uncomfortable or bring him bad news.

Paul's challenges concerning Edge are more subtle than Alice's, but still understandable in light of dynamics related to his personality type. His overuse of his preferred strategy caused him to exhibit both extremes of behavior related to Edge. In an effort to maintain an inner peacefulness he sometimes resisted conflict by soft-pedaling on issues that needed decisiveness. This behavior caused frustration among the people around him. Their frustration led them to push Paul harder for clarity. Unable to ignore the pushing anymore, Paul would lash out in order to end the discussion and move to a different topic.

Paul's challenge was to learn that his "peacefulness" was increased when he was decisive and "edgier" earlier in an engagement. He found that a small confrontation now would help avoid bigger conflicts down the road.

Paul also worked on his tendency to self-deprecate. This behavior—unnecessarily diverting credit or praise away from himself and minimizing his abilities and contributions (even to himself)—subtly undermined his authority and caused him to delay making decisions. His self-deprecation stemmed from his discomfort with "striving to be outstanding;" he believed that *appearing* to feel confident in himself or promote himself would cause him to seem arrogant or obnoxious. He worked with his coach to identify behaviors that were balanced between arrogance and false-humility, and his confidence (and appearance of confidence) began to grow. Soon, others also felt a renewed sense of confidence in Paul.

In many ways, the growth path is more challenging when one is underperforming in a competency than when one is over-performing in the same competency. Correcting over-performance often requires developing the habit of scaling back on a behavior, while correcting underperformance often requires learning and becoming proficient at new skills. Thus, Nines may have a tougher time around a competency like "Edge" than an Eight might, but they can make great progress in a relatively short time if they stay focused on the use or misuse of the Strategies and modify a few simple behaviors.

In order to be useful in business, a consultant's model of the Enneagram must be simple—focused on fundamental themes rather than detailed and laborious lists of traits or maze of psychodynamics. This is not to suggest that the leadership-development work that executives such as Alice and Paul are undertaking is easy—it is not. Change and growth are hard work. A simple and focused model of the Enneagram combined with a model of leadership competencies, however, makes that work easier.

The Strategies and Sales Competencies

We also apply the Enneagram to sales training. We created a competency model based on the five steps of the selling process, which are *Opening, Probing, Presenting, Answering Objections, and Closing*. These steps are fairly generic and nothing new, and some sales trainers reduce them to four steps or expand them to six or seven; other trainers change the order somewhat. The sales

213

competencies are similar to the emotional competencies described in this book, such as communication, initiative, and achievement drive, and some are subsets or more specific descriptions of these, such as assertiveness, focus, analytical skills, likeability, and so forth. Someone who is familiar with both the nine types and these five steps can easily predict which personality types will excel and which will struggle with each step. By contrast, the leadership competencies described above are broader categories and do not lend themselves to this sort of strength/weakness predictability based on type. For example, one could not say which personality type would excel in *Energize*, one of the leadership competencies; it would be more of a question of *how or in what style or manner*, a certain type accomplished this competency rather than *how well*.

In creating the sales competency model, we described the activities involved in each step, then described the competencies required to accomplish the activities in that step, as follows:

Step One: Opening activities involve introducing yourself and your company; building rapport, engaging in small talk, establishing the objective of your call, identifying the benefit of your visit and your product so that the customer will want to listen and participate. *Opening competencies* are friendliness and sociability, making a connection with the prospect, being a good listener, sharing, openness, responsiveness, likeability, and being relaxed while being direct and professional.

Step Two: Probing activities involve asking questions to uncover the prospect's needs and receptivity to your product or service. *Probing competencies* are curiosity, good questioning and listening skills, patience, analytical skills, staying focused on the prospect's needs, and the courage to respond to negative responses.

Step Three: Presenting activities involve talking about details and introducing the features and benefits of your product or service, how they meet the prospect's needs, and how they are superior to the product or services of the competition. *Presenting competencies* are product knowledge, focus on details, customer knowledge, being prepared, honesty, being a dynamic, systematic, professional presenter; the ability to think spontaneously and creatively in order to connect benefits to needs, and the persistence to probe for acceptance.

Step Four: Handling Objections activities involve acknowledging that the prospect's objection is important; questioning until you understand the "real" objection; answering the objection openly and directly, and confirming your answer to ensure the prospect accepts it. *Handling Objections competencies* are staying grounded and unruffled, handling conflict and rejection, staying objective and positive, staying focused on facts, being persist in probing, and persuasiveness—getting the prospect's commitment.

Step Five: Closing activities involve summarizing the prospect's needs and how your product or service satisfies them; emphasizing the major benefits and net gain of your product or service; supporting the benefits the prospect has agreed to; requesting the prospect's commitment, then waiting for an answer; managing any resistance or objections and asking again for commitment. *Closing competencies* are staying focused on the prospect's needs rather than yours, summarizing with precision; the discipline and discretion not to say *too* much; the assertiveness and confidence to request commitment, persistence in probing and answering any resistance; and the resilience to keep asking for the commitment.

In training sessions we videotape simulated sales calls and review them with sales trainees. Before viewing the tapes most salespeople are not aware that they consistently skip a step, or spend an inordinate amount of time on another step, are aggressive during one step, and passive or withdrawn during another. Again and again we observe how the sales person's behavior is consistently predictable based on personality type, and how this simple exercise can reveal sales derailers and help improve selling skills.

To illustrate this process, let's observe a video tape of Harry, a Type Two, and a computer software sales person in training. The Two's strategy is *striving to be connected.* Throughout all five steps of the sales process, we watch Harry striving to be connected. During the *Opening,* when building rapport, creating a relaxed atmosphere, and being likeable are key behaviors, Harry shines. During the *Probing* step, he does a good job because he can focus on the prospect, he's curious about the prospect and he's a good listener. When Harry gets into *Presenting,* he needs to shift more to product details and how his software meets the prospect's needs. However, for reasons unknown to Harry, he prefers to linger longer in the *Opening* step, where rapport has been established and a connection has been made. It's presentation time and the prospect is waiting to hear about the capabilities of the software, its price, warranty, deliverability and so forth. Harry is still making great eye contact, and trying to be pleasant and likeable. However, as Twos tend to do at this step in the sales process, Harry overuses connecting, does not focus on the product, does not break eye contact and draw the prospect's attention to the product or its spec sheet. We observe Harry describe the product's benefits, but he neglects to present some important technical data crucial to the prospect. By comparison, another type, such as a Five, who is focused more on facts and figures, and who can more naturally detach from the prospect and focus on the product, may be more effective during this step.

As the sales process moves from *Presenting* to *Handling Objections,* Harry enters an area of discomfort. The prospect has questions or objections that need to be addressed, and Harry's natural skills such as being connected, pleasant and complimentary aren't nearly as important as being decisive, confident, and knowledgeable. Harry appears uncomfortable with a challenging question about compatibility with existing software, and we observe Harry avoid the question and make a complimentary reference to the prospect's "great" company and how he has done business with them in the past. The prospect wants his question answered; Harry, however, wants to be liked. By contrast, Eights will usually be more effective at handling objections because of their natural skills of confidence, assertiveness, and the ability to anticipate and welcome challenges.

When we get to the *Closing* step, we observe another area where Harry needs to improve. Remember that the Two's strategy is striving to be connected. The prospect seems ready to make a commitment. He has asked when Harry can deliver the product. It's time for the close, but Harry keeps talking; he is rehashing the sales call from the beginning and running the risk of bringing up objections raised by the prospect that Harry has not addressed. Why isn't Harry closing the sale? One reason may be nerves, but as we have observed repeatedly with Twos, Harry may unconsciously feel that closing means saying good-bye to the prospect and losing the connection that he is hard-wired to maintain. Many Twos like Harry continue to "sell" the prospect after they've gotten a commitment to buy, and risk losing the sale because of it. Harry leaves the training session with an eye-opening view of where he needs to focus his attention, a rationale for why he, as a Two salesperson, does what he does, and a clear action plan for improvement.

This approach is powerful in sales training and coaching because it makes many unconscious behaviors conscious. It helps salespeople see their blind spots, rationalizations, and sales derailers. It teaches the power and synergy of applying all five steps of the sales process rather than just the ones salespeople are good at, or remember, or are comfortable with.

The Enneagram can be used effectively with any competency model in any organization.

BIBLIOGRAPHY

Almaas, A.H., *Facets of Unity*, Diamond Books, 1998.

Argyris, Chris, *Knowledge in Action*, Jossey-Bass, 1993.

Argyris, Chris, *Overcoming Organizational Defenses*, Allyn and Bacon, 1990.

Autry, James, *Love and Profit*, William Morrow, 1991.

Block, Peter, *The Empowered Manager,* Jossey-Bass, 1987.

Boyatzis, R.E., *The Competent Manager: A Model for Effective Performance*, New York: John Wiley and Sons, 1982.

Boyatzis. R. E., *Developing Emotional Intelligence*, Working Paper Series. Casc Western Reserve University, 1999.

Buckingham, Marcus, and Curth Coffman, *First Break All the Rules,* Simon and Shuster, 1999.

Burns, David, D., *Feeling Good,* Signet, 1980.

Canfield, Jack, Mark Victor Hansen, and Les Hewitt, *The Power of Focus,* Health Communications, Inc., 2000.

Chen, W. and Jacobs, R., *Competence Study*. Hay/McBer, Boston, MA, 1997.

Cialdini, Robert, *Influence, The Psychology of Persuasion,* Quill, 1993.

Conger, Jay, *Learning to Lead*, Jossey-Bass, 1992.

Conger, Jay, A., and Gretchen M. Spreitzer, and Edward F. Lawler, *Leader's Change Handbook*, Jossey-Bass, 1999.

Connor, Daryl, R, *Managing At the Speed of Change*, Villard Books, 1993.

Collins, James, and Jerry Porras, *Built to Last,* Harper Business, 1994.

Collins, Jim, *Good To Great,* Harper Business, 2001.

Covey, Stephen, *The 7 Habits of Highly Successful People,* Simon and Schuster, 1989.

Damasio, Antonio, *Descartes' Error*, Quill, 1994.

Dotlich, David, and Peter Cairo, *Action Coaching*, Jossey-Bass, Inc. 1999.

Ellis, Albert, and Blau Shawn, *The Albert Ellis Reader,* Citadel Pres, 1998.

Fritz, Robert, *The Path of Least Resistance*, Fawcett Columbine, 1989.

Goldberg, Michael, *Getting Your Bosses Number,* Harper San Franciso, 1996.

Goleman, Daniel, *Emotional Intelligence,* Bantam Books, 1995.

Goleman, Daniel, *Working With Emotional Intelligence*, Bantam Books, 1998.

Hargrove, Robert, *Masterful Coaching,* Jossey-Bass, 1995.

Horney, Karen, *Our Inner Conflicts,* W.W. Norton and Company, 1945.

Huber, Cheri, *There Is Nothing Wrong With You,* Keep It Simple Books, 1993.

Kaplan, Robert E., *Beyond Ambition*, Jossey-Bass, 1991.

Keirsey, David, and Marilyn Bates, *Please Understand Me, Character and Temperament Types,* Prometheus Nemesis Book Company, 1984.

Jones, John, and William Bearley, *360 Degree Feedback, Strategies, Tactics, and Techniques for Developing Leaders*, HRD Press, 1996.

Kegan, Robert, and Lisa Laskow Lahey, *How The Way We Talk Can Change the Way We Work*, Jossey-Bass, 2001.

Klein, Mermom, and Rod Napier, *The Courage to Act,* Davis Black Publishing, 2003.

Kouzes, James, and Barry Posner, *The Leadership Challenge,* Jossey-Bass, 1995.

Kotter, John, P. *A Force For Change,* The Free Press, 1990.

Langer, Ellen, J., *Mindfulness,* Perseus Books, 1989.

Leonard, George, *Mastery,* Dutton, 1991.

Maitri, Sandra, *The Spiritual Dimension of the Enneagram*, Jeremy Tarcher, 2000.

Miller, William, R. and Janet C'de Baca, *Quantum Change*, The Guilford Press, 2001.

Naranjo, Claudio, *Transformation Through Insight,* Hohm Press, 1997.

Naranjo, Claudio, *Enneatype Structures*, Gateways, 1990.

Naranjo, Claudio, *Character and Neurosis*, Gateways, 1996.

Naranjo, Claudio, *Enneatypes in Psychotherapy,* Hohm Press, 1995.

Osborn, Carol, M., *Inner Excellence at Work,* American Management Association, 2000.

Palmer, Helen, and Paul B. Brown, *The Enneagram Advantage,* Harmony Books, 1997.

Riso, Don Richard, and Russ Hudson, *Discovering Your Personality Type,* Revised, Houghton Mifflin, 2003.

Riso, Don Richard, and Russ Hudson, *Personality Types,* Revised, Houghton Mifflin, 1996.

Riso, Don Richard, and Russ Hudson, *The Wisdom of the Enneagram,* Bantam Books, 1999.

Rosier, R.. (ed.), *The Competency Model Handbook*, Volumes 1-3. Lexington: Linkage, 1996.

Schein, Edgar, *Process Consultation: Its Role in Organizational Development*, Addison-Wesley, 1969.

Senge, Peter, *The Fifth Discipline Fieldbook,* A Currency Book, 1994.

Scarfalloto, Rodolfo, *The Alchemy of Opposites,* New Falcon Publications, 1997.

Simon, Sidney, *Getting Unstuck,* Warner Books, 1988.

Tallon, Andrew, *Head and Heart*, Fordham University Press 1997.

Valentino, Albert, *Personality Selling,* Vantage Point, 2000.

Waldroop, James, and Timothy Butler, *Maximum Success,* Currency. Doubleday, 2000.

Wagner, Jerome, *The Enneagram Spectrum of Personality Styles,* Metamophous Press, 1996.

Weisinger, Henry, *Emotional Intelligence at Work*, Jossey-Bass, 1998.

Welch, Jack, with Suzy Welch, *Winning*, Harper Business, 2005

INDEX

ABOUT THE AUTHORS

Robert Tallon and **Mario Sikora** are consultants who have taught the Enneagram to business people since 1991. They have provided executive coaching, leadership development, team building, and sales training to organizations including Motorola, Johnson & Johnson, Rohm and Haas, Beazer Homes, IMS Health, Lincoln Investment Planning, Inc., the US Department of Agriculture, Comcast Cellular Communications, North American Title Insurance Company, Gift of Life Donor Program, Binney and Smith, and Quaker City Chemicals. Robert has two children and lives with his wife, Robyn, in Blue Bell, Pennsylvania, a suburb of Philadelphia. He can be reached at robert@awarenesstoaction.com.

Mario lives in Philadelphia, Pennsylvania, with his wife Tanya and their sons, Adrian, Alec and Alexie. He can be reached at mario@awarenesstoaction.com.